CAMPAIGN FINANCE REFORM

Other titles in the
Beyond the Basics series

BEYOND the BASICS

CAMPAIGN FINANCE REFORM

ANTHONY CORRADO

A CENTURY FOUNDATION BOOK

2000 ✳ THE CENTURY FOUNDATION PRESS ✳ NEW YORK

bpf 8388-6/1

The Century Foundation, formerly the Twentieth Century Fund, sponsors and supervises timely analyses of economic policy, foreign affairs, and domestic political issues. Not-for-profit and nonpartisan, it was founded in 1919 and endowed by Edward A. Filene.

LIBRARY OF CONGRESS CATALOGING-IN-PUBLICATION DATA

Corrado, Anthony, 1957–
    Campaign finance reform / Anthony Corrado.
        p. cm.
    Includes bibliographical references and index.
    ISBN 0-87078-432-3
    1. Campaign funds—United States. 2. Campaign funds—Law and legislation—United States. I. Title.
    JK1991 .C667 2000
    324.7'8'0973—dc21

00-009974

Cover design, graphics, and illustrations: Claude Goodwin
Manufactured in the United States of America.

FOREWORD

For decades, the Federal Reserve has been raising interest rates to curtail inflation, but there is one market where the strategy has not paid off at all. Increases in the "price" of a political campaign have grown at a pace far faster than the consumer price index, and there is no end in sight.

Every year, reformers lament this pattern and renew their calls for a variety of plans designed to reduce the influence of big money on American politics. From time to time, they have some successes, but the fruits of these small victories always seem to wither away as the rising cost of modern campaigning provokes new tactics for circumventing the system. Thanks in large part to a set of Supreme Court decisions that seem strangely disconnected from the reality of contemporary politics, there are, today, no restraints on spending by rich candidates, no real curbs on expensive "advocacy" campaign spending, and no effective limits on the use of so-called soft money— money contributed not directly to candidates but to other politically active organizations. The result of this free-for-all, for candidates and office holders, is a world in which the cultivation and solicitation of an endless stream of interest groups and wealthy individuals has come to occupy larger and larger portions of their time.

A senator from a major state needs to raise about $20,000 a week for an entire six-year term in order to finance a reelection effort. This year's primary campaign in New Jersey showed again just how potent a wealthy candidate willing to spend big could be. For most candidates, soliciting direct contributions to their campaigns is just the tip of the fundraising iceberg. They find themselves working even harder, within the existing, loose rules, to hustle contributions from large soft money donors and spending even more time assisting in the supplemental fundraising for party organizations and "coordinated campaigns." Pundits talk about the "Endless Campaign," but for those in public life, the term closer to the truth is the "endless hunt for money."

The green paper chase has become a way of life for all too many of our "representatives" in Washington. Some of them have even come to view the funding class as "typical" of America. But, of course, such large individual donors are an elite group—only one-tenth of 1 percent give more than $1,000 to federal candidates. They live in a rarefied political environment. Together with the large players from businesses, labor, and other interest groups, these contributors, unlike most citizens, find it pretty easy to be heard in Washington.

There are those, of course, who see nothing wrong with the escalating cost of campaigns and with the growing obsession with fundraising. Most citizens, however, take a dimmer view of the process, believing that nothing can be done to improve it. The stream of news reports about various accusations of fundraising abuses has fed the widespread cynicism about politics generally. In that climate, perhaps it is not surprising that various campaign finance reform efforts have failed to receive sufficient congressional support.

One fascinating development during the 2000 campaign has been the new role of the Internet in generating campaign contributions. After Republican presidential candidate John McCain won the New Hampshire primary, for example, he quickly raised $1.7 million over the Internet and ultimately collected $7 million over the course of his campaign. About 40 percent of those who contributed over the Internet had never before donated to a political campaign. Because the campaign finance laws have not adapted fully to the advent of the Internet, a whole new set of loopholes beyond those summarized in these pages has evolved—many of which are not yet well understood and remain to be exploited more fully.

The Century Foundation has a substantial track record in research and writing about campaign finance issues. Those works include the collection of essays *If Buckley Fell: A First Amendment Blueprint for Regulating Money in Politics; Buckley Stops Here: Loosening the Judicial Stranglehold on Campaign Finance Reform,* the report of a working group on campaign finance litigation; *Paying for Presidents,* Anthony Corrado's earlier report for The Century Foundation; Frank Sorauf's background paper for the Twentieth Century Fund Task Force on Political Action Committees, *What Price PACs?;* Herbert

Alexander's *Reform and Reality: The Financing of State and Local Campaigns*; and
Brooks Jackson's *Broken Promise: Why the Federal Election Commission Failed*.

During the 2000 election season, campaign finance reform remains a
prominent issue and may become newsworthy again in 2001 with a new
administration and Congress. Unfortunately, the debate over campaign finance
reform all too often has been characterized by inaccuracies and misleading
information. The purpose of this publication, written by Colby College professor of government Anthony Corrado, is to assemble essential facts and clar-
ify often confusing details about the subject. The report provides an overview
for nonexperts of campaign finance law, facts about the costs of campaigning
and sources of funding, the presidential public financing system, party financing and soft money, and issue advocacy. Finally, it explains various options
for reform while assessing their strengths and weaknesses.

We thank Corrado for his effort to show exactly why the campaign
finance system needs to be fixed and why it will be so difficult to repair.

RICHARD C. LEONE, *President*
The Century Foundation
June 2000

CONTENTS

1

INTRODUCTION

I s the campaign finance system out of control? Does money have too much influence in our political system? Is it corrupting government? Is it discouraging competition in elections for our nation's highest offices? Have the rules governing campaign finance been rendered meaningless by the rise of soft money, issue advocacy advertising, and other innovations in political funding? Is it possible to restrict the flow of money in campaigns without infringing on First Amendment freedoms or other liberties? And if the latter is possible, what changes are needed to bring about effective reform? These are the questions that frame the campaign finance debate. They are questions that speak to the health of our democracy, questions that every citizen should consider thoughtfully. And they are questions that become more pressing with each new election cycle.

The American people certainly believe that the campaign finance system is out of control. Most opinion surveys conducted in recent years show that from 70 to 90 percent of the public feel that the system is broken, and significant majorities think that money has too much influence in our political process. These public perceptions are a response to a number of alarming trends that have come to define the role of money in politics for most Americans: sharply rising campaign costs, a widening financial gap between incumbents and challengers, the increasing role of organized interests as

1

sources of campaign funding, and the growing influence of unlimited "soft money" contributions and other financial schemes that are designed to avoid the restrictions of federal law.

Although these trends have been evident for some time, the Federal Election Campaign Act (FECA), the major law governing the financing of federal campaigns, has not been amended since 1979. Since then, the flow of money in political campaigns has changed dramatically. Court decisions, Federal Election Commission rulings, and changing political practices have transformed the campaign finance system, often in unexpected and unintended ways. The resulting system is more a product of accident than design, a system that has expanded instead of restricted the amount of money involved in federal campaigns. Consequently, the FECA has failed to accomplish many of the goals that Congress hoped to achieve when it passed the law. In fact, the system has come almost full circle, evolving to a point where the contributions and expenditures that were supposed to be banned by the reforms of the 1970s once again have become commonplace.

THE FUNDRAISING FRENZY OF 1996

One need look no further than the 1996 election to understand the extent of the problems that bedevil the campaign finance system. The final weeks of the presidential campaign were dominated by allegations of improper and illegal fundraising by the Democrats. News agencies reported that the Democratic National Committee (DNC) had received millions of dollars in contributions from illegal foreign sources or from other questionable donors. Subsequent news reports revealed that some of the largest donors to the Democratic Party had been invited to the White House, and many had stayed overnight in the Lincoln Bedroom or attended one of a series of private coffees with the president. These revelations sparked a public furor over the possibility of the White House being up for sale and ignited the most widespread investigation into campaign fundraising since the Watergate scandal in 1972.

By the late spring of 1997, the Senate Governmental Affairs Committee, the Department of Justice, and the Federal Election Commission had launched formal investigations into party fundraising practices, and the House of Representatives had approved an inquiry of its own. In response to these investigations, the DNC was forced to admit that it indeed had received at least $3 million in contributions from illegal or questionable sources, and the party returned all of these funds to the donors. The White House released documents that showed that the president had attended 103 coffees with political supporters and donors, who contributed a total of more than $25 million to the Democrats in 1996. The documents also showed that the vice president had made a number of fundraising phone calls from his office, seeking contributions for the DNC in amounts of $50,000 or more.[1] These admissions, as well as information uncovered by the Senate investigation into the Democrats' 1996 fundraising practices, raised questions as to whether the president, vice president, or other administration officials might have violated federal campaign spending limits and the laws that prohibit fundraising by federal officials on government property. They also provoked broader concerns about the propriety of party fundraising practices, the special privileges being awarded to major donors and the influence of wealthy contributors on administration decisionmaking.

While the controversy centered on the president and the Democrats, public documents indicated that both parties had engaged in controversial fundraising practices during the 1996 campaign. Both parties raised tens of millions of dollars from individual donors in amounts that greatly exceeded the limit on contributions to party committees established by federal law. The national party committees also solicited gifts of $100,000 or more from corporations and labor unions, two sources that had long been banned from making contributions to federal campaigns. Much of this money, known as "soft money" because it is not subject to federal contribution limits, went to pay for television ads that were designed to benefit each party's presidential and congressional candidates. These ads then were scripted in a way that allowed the parties to circumvent federal restrictions on party spending. In effect, the parties had found ways to raise and spend unlimited amounts of money, which intensified the demand for dollars and heightened the stakes in the money race.

These sensational stories and subsequent inquiries associated with party fundraising activities often masked the broader—and more enduring—financial problems that are at the center of the campaign finance debate. Overall, the candidates, party organizations, and political committees involved in federal elections spent a record $2.7 billion, approximately $500 million more than the amount they spent in 1992.[2] To raise this record sum, candidates and the organizations that support them became engaged in a frenzied money chase. Members of Congress began soliciting money for their 1996 reelection campaigns soon after the 1994 elections. Many U.S. Senate candidates sought to raise $50,000 or more *every week* to generate the millions of dollars needed for their campaigns. Often they turned to organized interest groups for help in filling their campaign coffers, and in 1996 the political action committees (PACs) sponsored by these groups responded by contributing unprecedented amounts to federal candidates. Most of this money went to incumbents, helping them to outspend their opponents by more than two to one. Thus, armed with superior resources, almost all of the incumbents who sought reelection were returned to office.

REKINDLING THE DEBATE

The race for dollars in 1996 reinvigorated the recurring debate in Congress over campaign finance reform. Since 1986, Congress had considered legislation to address the problems of campaign funding with little success. In 1988, a two-year effort to reform the system by limiting the role of PACs and establishing a system of public subsidies and spending ceilings for House and Senate races failed as a result of a Republican-led Senate filibuster. In 1992, the Democratic-controlled House and Senate passed a similar bill, only to see it fail as a result of a veto by then-President George Bush. In 1993, each house passed its own version of a reform bill, which centered on PAC limits, curbs on soft money, and voluntary public subsidies and spending limits, but no conference was appointed by the end of the year, and an attempt to revive the proposals in 1994 fell before another Senate filibuster. Then, in 1996, with the Republicans now forming the majority in the House and Senate, Senators John McCain (R-Arizona) and Russell Feingold (D-Wisconsin) sponsored a bipartisan reform plan in an effort to break the partisan deadlock in Congress. This effort also was defeated by a Republican-led filibuster, falling six votes short of the sixty needed to end debate.[3]

At first it appeared that the prospects for reform would be different in the 105th Congress that convened in 1997. The furor over the financing of the 1996 campaign suggested that Congress was entering another cycle of scandal and reform, similar to that which had produced the FECA after Watergate and earlier legislation in 1925 after the Teapot Dome scandal. In addition, the Congress, which was still controlled by the Republicans, now included a group of more than two dozen freshmen members from both sides of the aisle who were advocates of reform and formed their own Bipartisan Task Force to consider ways of revising the system. Finally, the focus of the debate was changing. McCain and Feingold narrowed the scope of their reform proposal to focus on the unregulated forms of funding that had mushroomed in 1996—soft money and issue advocacy. A similar bipartisan bill was sponsored in the House by Representatives Christopher Shays (R-Connecticut) and Martin Meehan (D-Massachusetts). No longer was the debate about the role of PACs or the need for spending limits in congressional races. Now the discussion centered around the need to limit soft money, restrict issue advocacy expenditures, and improve disclosure. Advocates of reform thought that this agenda was more likely to be approved by Congress, since it avoided the major proposals (spending limits and public funding) that were the foundation of partisan gridlock in prior years.

While approximately eighty-five reform bills were submitted in 1997, ranging from complete deregulation of the system to a proposal for full public financing of campaigns, the leading alternatives were the McCain-Feingold bill (and its companion Shays-Meehan in the House) and a plan crafted by the House freshmen—the so-called Freshman bill.[4] The Senate took the lead, beginning consideration of the McCain-Feingold bill in the fall of 1997. Most Republicans opposed McCain-Feingold, arguing that its attempt to end soft money would undermine the role of political parties and that its restrictions on issue advertising were unconstitutional infringements on the First Amendment's guarantee of free speech. The Republicans, who were upset over the issue advertising sponsored by the AFL-CIO on behalf of Democrats during the 1996 elections, also sought to amend the proposal by adding a "paycheck protection" provision that would have required labor unions to get written permission from members before spending any treasury funds on political activity. The provision was designed to kill the bill, since it was anathema to Democrats and caused them to mount their own filibuster against the amendment. The Republicans failed to impose cloture on the debate over their amendment. Similarly, the Democrats lacked the votes needed to impose cloture against a Republican filibuster on the bill itself. In October 1997, advocates of reform failed to defeat a Republican filibuster on three separate occasions. While a majority of the Senate supported McCain-Feingold, the reformers could not muster the sixty votes needed to pass the bill.

The House, however, was not willing to give up the fight. Supporters of Shays-Meehan and the Freshman bill continued to push for a vote. The Republican leadership tried to circumvent these efforts by unexpectedly scheduling a vote on four leadership-backed bills in March under an unusual use of the suspension of the rules procedure. The bills called for relatively minor changes compared to Shays-Meehan, and two of the four were defeated as reformers decried what they considered a "mockery" and a "sham." The two that did pass simply called for a ban on contributions by noncitizens and stronger disclosure rules. Neither of these were adopted by the Senate.

Frustrated by the lack of action on a major reform bill, reformers gave new life to a discharge petition that would dislodge the Shays-Meehan bill from committee and place it before the floor for a vote. By April 21, the petition had gathered 204 signatures, including 12 Republicans, and was only 14 signatures short of the 218 needed to force a vote. House Speaker Newt Gingrich responded by agreeing to bring the bill to the floor in May.[5]

When the House finally began floor debate on campaign finance reform on May 21, it did so under a procedure that allowed eleven different bills to be considered, with the bill gathering the most votes to be the one approved by the House. The procedure also called for the Freshman bill to be considered first, thus pitting its supporters against the supporters of Shays-Meehan. Moreover, the procedure allowed multiple amendments, and eventually the bills faced 258 amendments that were ultimately trimmed down to 55 amendments.[6] During the ten weeks of debate that followed, all of the Republican amendments were defeated, as was the Freshman bill, and in August the Shays-Meehan proposal was approved by a vote of 252-179, with sixty-one Republicans joining all but fifteen Democrats.

With majorities in both the House and Senate now having expressed support for Shays-Meehan or McCain-Feingold, advocates of this reform plan thought that the Senate now would reconsider its position and the additional votes to secure passage in the Senate would be achieved. But in early September, when the Senate took up Shays-Meehan, no major shift in voting occurred. Once again the Senate Republicans mounted a filibuster, and the vote fell eight short of invoking cloture. A minority thus managed to dash the best prospect for bipartisan reform in more than a decade.

In the 106th Congress, the reformers again brought up campaign finance reform legislation, with the hope that the intervening election of 1998 and the prospect of the election of 2000 might encourage some shift in legislative attitudes. The House again considered the Shays-Meehan bill, now H.R. 417, and passed it in September 1999. But the margin and voting patterns were essentially no different than those in the previous Congress. The House voted for the bill by a margin of 252-177, which represented the same level of support as in 1998. The partisan divide on the issue was actually greater than that of the previous Congress, as only 54 Republicans approved of the measure (164 opposed it), which was 7 fewer than in 1998. The House again had produced a majority in favor of reform, but as in the previous Congress, this effort would not be enough to produce new regulations.

In the upper house, Senators McCain and Feingold tried to improve the prospects for their bill by stripping the issue advocacy provisions and focusing primarily on soft money. The reformers thought that a straight vote on a soft money ban or a soft money ban with amendments might be more appealing to Republican members or, at least, would be more difficult to vote against. This tactic, however, did little to change the dynamic that has come to characterize Senate campaign finance deliberations in recent Congresses. The Republican leadership put forth alternative proposals, and Senator Mitch McConnell of Kentucky led a successful filibuster. In the end, the 106th Congress produced only one additional Republican vote for the McCain-Feingold proposal, as all forty-five Democrats were joined by eight Republicans, one more than in the previous Congress. The vote to cut off the filibuster failed by a margin of seven votes, 53-47. A subsequent vote on the more comprehensive version of McCain-Feingold that included the issue advocacy provisions failed by a margin of eight votes, 52-48. This vote marked the twentieth time since 1987 that Republican leaders had used a filibuster to scrap a campaign finance reform plan.[7]

MIXED MOTIVES

The 1996 elections and subsequent legislative debates highlight the problems that must be overcome to reform our campaign finance laws. Instead of clarifying the reform agenda, current trends in campaign funding and recent legislative proposals have served to increase the complexity of the issues involved in this debate, making reform that much more difficult to achieve. The regulation of political finance entails the regulation of political speech, which means that lawmakers must balance various policy objectives against the liberties guaranteed by the First Amendment. The objectives they seek often compete, with some policymakers seeking to limit a candidate's funding while others seek to expand a candidate's access to funds. Some want to expand the role of political parties while others want to restrict party financing. Some want to limit the sphere of regulation over political activity while others want to extend regulation to ensure that the laws cannot be circumvented.

The ideological and empirical preferences that underlie these diverse goals often give rise to partisan disputes over the nature of the problem and the efficacy of various solutions. Indeed, many of the fundamental policy ideas advanced in this debate have been marked by a partisan divide that even the most artful legislators have been unable to overcome. This barrier to reform often is reinforced by the self-interest of legislators, who have a stake in preserving the status quo. Incumbents are the beneficiaries of the current system, and any proposal to assist challengers would, by definition, make it more difficult for incumbents to win reelection. Incumbents thus tend to approach reform warily, giving due regard to the effects any proposal might have on their own campaign resources or on the resources available to prospective opponents.

One factor that would help generate greater legislative support is stronger public demand for reform. While vast majorities believe that change is needed, a relatively small share of the electorate rank this issue high enough to make it the basis of their vote. Even in 1998, well after the abuses of 1996 had been publicized and the problems of unregulated funding had become manifest, campaign finance was not a salient voting issue for most citizens. Legislators have less incentive to resolve an issue if they believe they will not suffer at the ballot box for a failure to act. Such public accountability is particularly important when it comes to campaign finance reform since the rules of procedure, especially in the Senate, function in such a way that a working majority is often not enough to secure passage of a piece of legislation.

The purpose of this book is to promote public awareness of the issues involved in the campaign finance debate. It reviews the federal laws governing campaign funding, provides an overview of the financial activity in recent elections, and details the most controversial aspects of the current system. It sets out the basic arguments raised about the current system and outlines the major reform alternatives, so that citizens may gain a better understanding of the current controversies over the role of money in politics.

2

An Overview of Campaign Finance Law

The regulation of federal campaign financing is governed by the provisions of the Federal Election Campaign Act (FECA). The FECA was first enacted in 1971, as a response to rising campaign costs and concerns about the role of money in congressional campaigns. This initial version of the law required public disclosure of campaign receipts and expenditures, placed limits on the sums candidates and their families could personally contribute to their campaigns, and set ceilings on the amount a candidate could spend on media.[1] In 1974, the FECA was substantially revised to address the issues raised by the Watergate scandal and other financial abuses disclosed after the 1972 presidential campaign. The 1974 FECA, which was modified in 1976 and 1979, is the basis of the current law.

The FECA created a comprehensive system to regulate the monies raised and spent in federal elections. Its primary purpose was to end the corruption or appearance of corruption that can accompany large, undisclosed contributions to candidates. Prior to the adoption of the law, the size and sources of candidate contributions were not publicly disclosed, and there were no effective limits on the amount of money that individuals or groups could contribute to federal campaigns. The FECA established contribution limits for

9

the different sources of funding in federal campaigns and required full public disclosure of contributions and expenditures.

The law also sought to control rising campaign costs and reduce the inequities in the resources available to candidates. To achieve these ends, the law imposed strict limits on the amounts that candidates, party committees, and political groups could spend. By capping expenditures, Congress hoped that costs could be brought under control and that the sizable differences in spending between candidates could be reduced substantially. These limits also were designed to increase the competitiveness of campaigns since they would equalize the resources available to candidates, which would make it more difficult for one candidate to seek victory simply by outspending an opponent by a large margin. Since a candidate could no longer spend as much as he or she could raise, the limits also were seen as a way to reduce the emphasis on fundraising in federal elections.

The FECA also reduced the emphasis on fundraising by creating a voluntary program of public financing for the most expensive election—the race for the White House. Heralded as the most innovative feature of the new law, the public subsidy program, which was financed through a checkoff on federal income tax forms, offered those seeking a party's presidential nomination the option of matching the amounts received from small individual contributions with public money on a dollar-for-dollar basis. The program also provided full public funding for the major party nominees in the general election, as well as a proportionate subsidy for qualified minor party candidates. This public funding option was designed to reduce the amount of money candidates had to raise on their own—and to give candidates an incentive to solicit small contributions. Congress hoped that this innovation would expand public participation in the financing of campaigns, which would help safeguard the electoral process against any undue influence on the part of a relatively small group of donors.

Finally, in order to ensure effective enforcement and administration of the law, Congress created a new, bipartisan administrative agency, the Federal Election Commission (FEC). Before the establishment of the FEC, there was no single organization responsible for enforcing campaign finance laws. There was no centralized administration, no public reporting of the limited information that was required by the laws on the books, and no enforcement of these laws. The FECA sought to remedy this situation by creating an independent commission and charging it with the responsibility for administering and enforcing the law.

This original conception of the FECA was never put into effect. Before the law could be implemented fully, it was challenged in the Supreme Court in the case of *Buckley* v. *Valeo*. The challenge was largely based on the argument that political contributions and expenditures are forms of political speech and therefore protected by the First Amendment. Thus any restraint on these activities would infringe on the freedom of speech. Supporters of the new law argued that the FECA's restrictions did not violate the First Amendment and were needed to protect the integrity of the electoral process. The Supreme Court's ultimate decision substantially changed the provisions of the FECA and had far-reaching consequences for the regulation of campaign finance.

HOW HAVE THE COURTS INFLUENCED CAMPAIGN FINANCE LAW?

In 1976, the Supreme Court issued its landmark decision on campaign finance regulation in the case of *Buckley* v. *Valeo*.[2] The Court struck down some of the major provisions of the FECA and set forth a number of basic rulings that govern policy in this area to this day. In general, the Court decided that campaign contributions and expenditures are forms of political speech protected by the First Amendment. As such, they only can be limited if there is a compelling reason to do so. In the view of the Court, restrictions are justified only if they serve the objective of reducing corruption—any quid pro quos that might accompany campaign donations—or the appearance of corruption. The Court rejected other rationales, including the desire to equalize the resources available to candidates, as insufficient to justify restrictions on free speech. The Court further noted that in attempting to prevent corruption or the appearance of corruption, Congress could not impose limits that were so severe that they starved campaigns or blocked individuals' ability to show their support for the candidates of their choice.

The Court in *Buckley* thus significantly limited the scope of permissible regulation. It upheld the disclosure provisions and contribution limits established by the FECA, arguing that these provisions serve the purpose of guarding against corruption or the appearance of corruption while constituting marginal restrictions on a donor's political speech since it is the act of contributing more than the amount contributed that represents a donor's expression of support. But the Court struck down most of the limits on expenditures. It ruled that caps on spending impose a much greater restriction on speech than caps on contributions, and that spending limits were not essential for the prevention of corruption since this purpose could be achieved through disclosure and contribution limits. It therefore deemed unconstitutional the law's limits on the amount candidates may spend personally on their campaigns, the cap on the amount an individual or group may spend independently on behalf of a candidate, and the ceiling on the total amount a candidate may spend.[3] In the Court's view, the only allowable ceilings were the voluntary ceilings imposed on presidential candidates who voluntarily accepted them as a condition of public financing. Absent public funding (or some other benefit), limits on spending are unconstitutional restraints on free speech.

Furthermore, the Court's decision in *Buckley* significantly reduced the realm of political activity Congress could regulate. In adopting the FECA, Congress sought to control all contributions and expenditures made "in connection with" federal elections or made "relative to a clearly identified federal candidate." The Court, however, felt these conceptions were too vague and broad and allowed Congress too much leeway in regulating political speech. It therefore determined that the law's provisions would be applicable to expenditures that expressly advocate the election or defeat of a federal candidate. Campaign communications that do not meet this "express advocacy" requirement are not subject to the FECA's limits. In a footnote, the Court provided examples of messages that would meet this express advocacy standard. Included were messages that used words such as "vote for," "elect," "support," "defeat," or "Smith for Congress."[4] Other messages, including messages that only provide information about a candidate, publicize a candidate's voting record, or contain information about issues, would not meet the standard and would not be subject to federal regulation.

The *Buckley* ruling created an imbalance in the FECA's regulatory scheme. While the Court upheld contribution limits, or controls on the supply of money, it did not allow most expenditure limits, or controls on the demand for money. Subsequent decisions by the Supreme Court and other federal courts have followed this basic approach and reaffirmed the Court's decision in *Buckley* that the FECA restrictions only would apply to political speech that expressly advocates the election or defeat of federal candidates.[5] The courts thus have permitted unlimited spending and opened the door to new approaches to campaign finance. But before examining the ramifications of these decisions, it is necessary to review the aspects of the law that have withstood judicial scrutiny.

WHAT ARE THE CONTRIBUTION LIMITS ESTABLISHED BY THE LAW?

The FECA places limits on the amounts that individuals, political committees, and party committees may donate to candidates and prohibits contributions from corporations, national banks, and labor unions. The law also prohibits contributions from foreign nationals, defined as foreign citizens who are not lawfully admitted for permanent residence in the United States. Foreign citizens who are permanent residents of the United States may make contributions in connection with federal elections. These limits and restrictions apply to anything of value given to a candidate or political committee either directly or in the form of some in-kind service. The limits thus apply to direct financial contributions, loans, and loan guarantees, as well as in-kind contributions of office space, equipment, fundraising expenses, salaries, and the like.

INDIVIDUALS. Individuals may contribute up to $1,000 per election, or a total of $2,000 ($1,000 in a primary and another $1,000 in the general election), to a candidate for federal office. Individuals may give up to $20,000 per year to a national party committee, such as the Republican National Committee or the Democratic National Committee. Additional limits include a cap of $5,000 per year on contributions to a political action committee and $5,000 per year on donations to a state party committee (which includes any donations to local party committees). All donations made by an individual in connection with federal elections also are subject to an annual aggregate limit of $25,000 per year. Thus, no individual may give a total of more than $25,000 in gifts to all federal candidates, party committees, and political action committees in any one year.

POLITICAL ACTION COMMITTEES. The limits imposed on political action committees (PACs) depend on whether a PAC qualifies as a multicandidate committee under the law. To qualify as a multicandidate committee, a PAC must be registered with the FEC for six months, receive contributions from at least fifty-one donors, and make contributions to at least five federal candidates. A multicandidate PAC may contribute up to $5,000 per election to a candidate, and up to $5,000 to other PACs each year. Additionally, a PAC can give up to $15,000 per year to a national party committee and a combined total of $5,000 to state or local party committees.

A PAC that does not have multicandidate status is considered a political committee and is limited to contributions of $1,000 to each candidate per election, but it may still give $5,000 per year to another PAC. These committees can, however, give more to a national party committee—$20,000 per year—than multicandidate PACs, but are subject to the same limit of $5,000 per year to state and local committees.

PARTY COMMITTEES. The law establishes different limits for party contributions in House and Senate races. Each national and state party committee can give $5,000 per election to a House candidate. In a Senate contest, the law sets a combined limit that restricts the national party committee and national senatorial campaign committee to a total contribution of $17,500. In addition, a state party committee can donate up to $5,000 to a Senate candidate. A party committee also can contribute $5,000 per year to a PAC. And there is essentially no restriction on the amount one party committee can give to another since the law allows party committees to "transfer funds" from one committee to another without limit. So, for example, a national party committee can transfer unlimited amounts of money to a federal congressional campaign committee or to a state or local party committee without violating the contribution limits.

CANDIDATES. A candidate for federal office may make unlimited contributions to his or her campaign from personal funds. The only limit on the use of personal funds is in the case of publicly financed presidential candidates, who are limited to $50,000 in contributions to their own campaigns under the terms of the public financing regulations (see Table 2.1, page 16).

WHAT ARE COORDINATED EXPENDITURES?

Contributing money to a candidate is by far the most common form of financial activity in federal elections. But the law also allows parties, groups, and individuals to spend money in other ways to help federal candidates. Congress acknowledged the unique role political parties play in the election process by allowing parties to supplement any direct contributions they make with expenditures made on *behalf of* individual candidates. These funds, because they are spent in coordination with candidates, are known as "coordinated expenditures."

As with direct contributions, coordinated expenditures can be made only from funds received under federal contribution limits. Coordinated expenditures differ from direct contributions, however, in that the party exercises some control over how the money is spent by working with candidates to make these decisions. For example, parties may assist candidates by conducting polls on their behalf, financing some of their media expenses, or doing research on an opponent. Another difference is that parties may make contributions to candidates in both a primary and a general election, but coordinated expenditures can be made only in connection with a candidate's general election campaign.

The FECA places ceilings on the amount a party committee may spend in coordination with a federal candidate. These ceilings are based on formulas established for each type of election at the federal level. Under the original terms set forth in 1974, national party committees could spend up to $10,000 per candidate in a House general election campaign, except in those states with only one congressional district, in which case the limit was $20,000. In

Senate general elections, the limit was the greater amount of $20,000 or two cents times the state's voting-age population, while the presidential election ceiling was simply two cents the voting-age population (or approximately $2.9 million in 1974). Each of these limits was indexed for inflation, so they have increased with each new election cycle. By 1996, they were roughly three times their original amounts. For example, national party committees could spend approximately $12 million on behalf of a presidential candidate. In 1998, the congressional limits were $32,550 for a House candidate ($65,100 in a single-district state), and from $65,100 in the smallest states to $1.5 million in California for Senate candidates.

State party committees are allowed to spend the same coordinated amounts in House and Senate races as the national party organizations. They are not allowed to spend coordinated amounts on the presidential race. Moreover, the so-called state party limit is actually the limit for state *and* local party organizations in a state; the law makes no separate provision for spending by county or local party organizations. In many instances, state parties transfer their spending authority to the national party committees since the state parties often lack the resources to finance the full amount allowed under the law and the national committees prefer to exercise centralized control over the coordinated disbursements. This transfer of authority is accomplished through a device known as an "agency agreement," which effectively doubles the amount a national committee can spend on behalf of a congressional candidate. In recent elections such agreements have become increasingly common, which has enhanced the role of national party organizations in the financing of congressional campaigns.

WHAT ARE INDEPENDENT EXPENDITURES?

Individuals and groups may not coordinate with a candidate when spending money on his or her behalf. If they do, any amount spent is considered a contribution subject to federal contribution limits. They can, however, spend money independently without contacting a candidate to advocate the election of the candidate or the defeat of an opponent. Such expenditures, known as "independent expenditures," are not limited with respect to their amounts, but all funds spent in this manner must come from contributions that are subject to federal contribution limits.

Independent spending can consist of a variety of different types of expenditure, ranging from the cost incurred by an individual or group when taking out an ad in a local newspaper to the costs of a political mailing or a television advertising campaign. In recent elections, independent expenditures have

TABLE 2.1
FEDERAL CONTRIBUTION LIMITS

DONORS	RECIPIENTS				SPECIAL LIMITS
	Candidate (or candidate committee)	Political Action Committee (multicandidate PAC^a)	State or Local Political Party (party committee)	National Political Party (party committee)	
INDIVIDUAL (or partnership)	$1,000 per election[b]	$5,000 per calendar year	$5,000 per calendar year[c] (combined limit on contributions to all state and local parties)	$20,000 per calendar year[c]	$25,000 per calendar year (combined limit on contributions to all candidates, PACs, and parties)
POLITICAL ACTION COMMITTEE (multicandidate PAC^a)	$5,000 per election[b]	$5,000 per calendar year	$5,000 per calendar year[c] (combined limit on contributions to all state and local parties)	$15,000 per calendar year[c]	—
CORPORATIONS AND LABOR UNIONS	prohibited	prohibited	unlimited by federal law provided money used for non-candidate-specific activities[d] (see also footnote c below)		—
STATE OR LOCAL POLITICAL PARTY (party committee)	$5,000 per election (combined limit on contributions to all candidates)	$5,000 per calendar year (combined limit on contributions to all PACs)	unlimited "transfers" to other party committees		—
NATIONAL POLITICAL PARTY[e] (party committee)	$5,000 per election[b]	$5,000 per calendar year	unlimited "transfers" to other party committees		$17,500 to a U.S. Senate candidate per campaign

^a Most business, labor, and ideological/issue PACs are "multicandidate" committees under federal law, which means they have been registered for at least six months, have at least fifty contributors, and have made contributions to at least five federal candidates. Non-multicandidate committees are subject to the same contribution limits as individuals.

^b Each primary and general election counts as a separate election.

^c This limit applies only to money used to support or oppose federal candidates. There are no federal limits on money that individuals and PACs can give to political parties for non-candidate-specific "party building" activities such as issue development, voter registration, and get-out-the-vote drives. Money used for these non-federally regulated purposes is called "soft money."

^d Some states impose their own limits on contributions to state and local parties, regardless of how the money is used.

^e Includes U.S. Senate and House of Representative campaign committees, as well as parties' national committees, each of which may contribute $5,000 to a candidate or PAC.

Source: Money in Politics: Reform Principles, Problems and Proposals (Washington, D.C.: Center for Responsive Politics, 1996).

---

usually taken the form of television or radio ads, or direct mailings that provide voters with information as to why they should vote for or against a candidate. Most of these expenditures have been made by PACs, which use independent spending as a means of providing additional assistance to candidates in excess of the amounts they are allowed to contribute.

The FECA originally limited independent spending to $1,000 per person or group, but the Supreme Court in *Buckley* ruled that individuals and political committees have the right to spend unlimited amounts of their own money to participate in the electoral process on an independent basis. If they do coordinate their activities, any amounts spent count as contributions subject to the limits of the law. All independent expenditures, whether made by individuals or organized groups, are subject to full public disclosure.

Corporations and labor unions are barred from making independent expenditures from the funds in their treasuries. This prohibition has been upheld by the courts on the basis that the expenditure of corporate or labor union funds in this manner poses a risk of corruption or may generate the appearance of corruption. As the Supreme Court has noted, this restraint on corporate and union speech is justified because it helps reduce the possibility of "the corrosive and distorting effects of immense aggregations of wealth that are accumulated with the help of the corporate form and that have little or no correlation to the public's support for the corporation's political ideas."[6]

Until 1996, political parties also were barred from making independent expenditures. Federal regulations assumed a relationship between a party and the candidates who run on a party's ticket, a relationship recognized by the special provisions for coordinated expenditures, and thus did not permit a party committee to spend additional sums on behalf of its candidates through independent expenditures. But in the Supreme Court's splintered decision in *Colorado Republican Federal Campaign Committee v. Federal Election Commission*,[7] a majority of judges ruled that party committees could make independent expenditures. Accordingly, in 1996, national party committees spent monies independently on behalf of their candidates for the first time. These expenditures were made by the national senatorial campaign committees, which disbursed more than $11 million in independent expenditures in connection with Senate contests. Most of this amount, about $9.7 million, was spent by the National Republican Senatorial Committee.[8]

One question left unanswered by the *Colorado* decision was whether Congress could constitutionally limit party spending. While the Supreme Court's decision opened the possibility of independent expenditures by party committees, it did not rule on the broader issue of the constitutionality of the ceilings imposed by the FECA on party-coordinated expenditures. The Supreme Court chose not to decide this issue in its initial *Colorado* ruling because a number of justices felt that additional argument and factual evidence might be relevant to the issues yet to be determined. So this portion of the case was sent back to the district court in Colorado for further proceedings on the constitutionality of the coordinated spending limits.

In 1998, the district court heard the case, which now reverted to its earlier title of *Federal Election Commission v. Colorado Republican Federal Campaign Committee*, since the FEC was the plaintiff in the original case. But the case came to be known more commonly as *Colorado II* in order to distinguish it from the parts of the case previously decided by the Supreme Court. The court reached a decision in February 1999, ruling that the coordinated spending limits that had been left standing after *Buckley* were unconstitutional. The opinion, citing *Buckley*, noted that the concern with corruption is related to "large individual financial contributions" and that party-coordinated expenditures "are not large individual contributions." The court further contended that the FEC failed to demonstrate that the coordinated spending limits served to limit corruption or were needed to prevent the types of quid pro quos or appearances of corruption that constitute the basis for acceptable restriction of political speech. Accordingly, the district court judge deemed the coordinated spending limits to be unconstitutional.[9]

The FEC appealed the district court decision in *Colorado II* soon after it was issued in an effort to preserve the coordinated spending limits. But in May 2000, the Court of Appeals in the Tenth Circuit in a 2-1 decision upheld the district court ruling and found the limits to be unconstitutional.[10] This opinion left the status of the regulations on coordinated spending as a matter of some uncertainty. At least in the Tenth Circuit, the limits are now considered unconstitutional, and parties may spend as much as they like in support of their candidates. The question is whether the same decision would be reached in other sections of the country or if it will be upheld by the Supreme Court. Party committees will face the choice of either relying on the Tenth Circuit decision to spend unlimited amounts in a coordinated manner elsewhere (thereby challenging the law on the books and assuming that any future court challenge will be successful) or deciding to continue to adhere to the limits pending further clarification. Or they might even rely on party committees within the Tenth Circuit as conduits to make unlimited coordinated expenditures throughout the country. Similarly, the FEC may face the question of whether to enforce the limits strictly in 2000 or wait for the outcome of the judicial review before making any final determination on compliance with the law.

ARE THERE EXEMPTIONS TO THE FECA'S RULES ON CONTRIBUTIONS AND EXPENDITURES?

CORPORATE AND LABOR UNION EXEMPTIONS

The FECA continues the long-standing ban against the use of corporate and labor treasury funds in federal elections (the corporate prohibition dates back to 1907 and the comparable labor prohibition to World War II). Corporations cannot use the monies generated from their business enterprises and held in their corporate bank accounts to make contributions to federal candidates. Similarly, labor unions may not use monies received from mandatory union member dues or from private enterprises for this purpose. If corporations and labor unions want to contribute funds to candidates or make independent expenditures, they must establish PACs. These PACs must rely on voluntary contributions from members, shareholders, and others to finance their activities in federal elections. There are, however, a couple of exemptions to this general rule since the FECA does permit the use of corporate and labor treasury funds in some forms of political finance.

PAC ADMINISTRATIVE COSTS. The first exemption in the prohibition against the use of treasury monies has to do with the costs of maintaining a PAC. If a corporation or labor union sponsors a PAC, it can pay for the PAC's administrative costs out of treasury funds; unlike other PACs, corporate and labor PACs do not have to pay administrative expenses out of the monies raised by the PAC. They also do not have to disclose publicly the total amounts spent on administrative costs.

INTERNAL COMMUNICATIONS EXEMPTION. Corporations and labor unions are allowed to spend unlimited amounts communicating with their own members or what the law defines as their "restricted class." For a corporation, this means unlimited communication with its stockholders and its executive and administrative personnel and their families. For unions, this means communication with members and their families. These "internal communications" may include messages that support or oppose specific candidates for federal office. While these communications are not generally regulated by the FEC, any spending on internal communications of $2,000 or more per election that expressly advocates the election or defeat of a candidate must be reported to the FEC.

Corporations and labor unions also can spend unlimited amounts from their treasury funds on nonpartisan political activity, such as voter registration drives and voter turnout programs. But these activities, at least with respect to labor unions, have usually been used to register and turn out voters in a partisan manner and on behalf of specific, endorsed candidates.

ISSUE ADVOCACY GROUP EXEMPTION. Finally, one category of corporations is exempt from the general rule regarding corporate independent expenditures. Since 1986, the Supreme Court has held that certain ideologically based nonprofit corporations, specifically those whose express purpose is to promote political ideas or policy issues, should be allowed to make independent expenditures in connection with federal elections.[11] Accordingly, the FEC has established criteria to determine which corporations qualify under this exemption. Essentially, the regulations state that a qualified corporation: (1) must have as its only express purpose the promotion of political ideas; (2) cannot engage in business activities other than raising funds for its own efforts; (3) must have no shareholders or other persons (beyond employees or creditors) who can make claims on the company's assets; and (4) cannot be established by a business corporation or labor organization.[12] Corporations that meet these criteria, which are usually ideological groups or organizations established to promote particular ideas—for example, some pro-life or abortion rights organizations or environmental groups—can make unlimited independent expenditures. As with other independent expenditures, these disbursements must be publicly disclosed to the FEC.

POLITICAL PARTY GENERIC ACTIVITY EXEMPTION

Although the FECA was designed to regulate all contributions and expenditures by political parties in federal elections, the law was amended in 1979 to exempt certain types of activity from the act's general prohibitions. This exemption arose as a result of the initial experience with the FECA in the

1976 election. Traditionally, parties have participated in federal election campaigns by financing voter registration drives, generic party advertising (messages like "Vote Democratic" or "Support the Republican Party"), and voter turnout programs, and by producing campaign materials, such as bumper stickers, slate cards, yard signs, and buttons. Although these activities and materials are not direct forms of assistance to particular federal candidates, they may *indirectly* benefit federal candidates by spreading a candidate's name or encouraging individuals to vote who otherwise might have stayed home.

Under the FECA's original guidelines, the costs of these party activities could be considered in-kind contributions (contributions of services or goods) to a candidate, which are subject to the FECA's contribution limits. This legal issue was a particular concern in the 1976 presidential race because the rules of the public financing program restricted presidential general election candidates to the amount of the public subsidy—they could not supplement this funding with additional monies received through contributions.[13] Party officials therefore had to rely on the presidential campaign committee for the money needed to finance campaign material and voter turnout drives. But both presidential campaigns were unwilling to devote significant sums of money to these purposes; since their funds were limited, they wanted to allocate as much as possible to media advertising. After the election, party leaders complained that the FECA had indirectly limited traditional grassroots and party-building activities and reduced the role of party organizations in the presidential campaigns.

Congress responded to these concerns by easing the restrictions on party contributions and expenditures. In 1979, the FECA was amended to exempt a set of very specific, narrowly defined grassroots and party activities from the definitions of "expenditure" and "contribution" contained in the act.[14] Specifically, parties were allowed to spend unlimited amounts of money on grassroots, party-building activities, such as voter registration and turnout drives. They also were allowed to spend unlimited sums on slate cards, sample ballots, brochures, posters, buttons, and bumper stickers for use in connection with volunteer campaign efforts. These materials could include the names of federal candidates as long as three or more candidates were listed. But none of these candidate lists could be distributed through public advertising, such as broadcast, newspaper, or billboard advertising since the purpose of the exemption was to promote public, grassroots participation in elections, not to provide parties with a means of undertaking additional candidate media advertising. Moreover, the 1979 reforms did not exempt parties from the contribution limits established by the law; the caps on contributions to party committees remained in place, but the expenditures made under this exemption were not to be considered contributions to the candidates who might benefit from these party activities.

WHAT ARE THE MAJOR AREAS OF CAMPAIGN FINANCE NOT COVERED BY THE FECA?

The FECA does not regulate all of the financial activity that takes place in federal elections. Judicial decisions and administrative rulings have placed some forms of contributing and spending outside the FECA's jurisdiction. In general, the law has been interpreted in a way that exempts certain activities from its contribution and expenditure limits because these efforts are not considered to be forms of campaign spending that expressly advocate the election or defeat of a specific federal candidate, which is the main criterion that defines the scope of federal regulation. These activities include party efforts that are designed to help build support for a party, such as general party advertising or voter registration drives, and communications that seek to educate the public about policy issues or candidate voting records. As a result, there are major areas of campaign finance that are not subject to the FECA's limits, even though these types of financing may benefit federal candidates or have a significant influence on the outcome of federal elections.

Two types of unregulated financial activity that have become especially prominent in recent years are party soft money and issue advocacy spending. These activities, which often are cast as major "loopholes" in the law by many advocates of campaign finance reform, actually encompass practices that have long been a part of election campaigns. But they have grown in prominence over the past decade as parties, interest groups, corporations, and labor unions have searched for methods of circumventing the FECA's restrictions or simply have looked for ways to play a more active role in electoral politics. Because court decisions and FEC rulings have sanctioned these activities and permitted certain types of unlimited funding, they have become the tactics of choice for those actors who are otherwise restricted under federal law. Consequently, soft money and issue advocacy have become major conduits for large sums of unlimited money. They are, by far, the most controversial aspects of the campaign finance system.

SOFT MONEY

About the same time that Congress was considering a revision of the FECA to allow parties greater freedom to spend money, the FEC was considering a related issue on party spending. The FECA regulations were based on the assumption that national party committees were involved primarily in federal election activity and therefore subject to federal regulation. Party officials, however, were making the case that the Democratic and Republican

National Committees also were involved in such nonfederal election activities as assisting state and local candidates or building party support at the state and local level. In addition, many of the generic activities the parties financed, such as voter registration drives and get-out-the-vote efforts, were conducted to help both federal and nonfederal candidates. This practical reality raised the question of whether these activities could be financed in part from monies raised under state law rather than the stricter contribution limits of federal law.

In 1978, the FEC decided that the monies spent on generic party activities, such as voter registration and turnout drives, and any party administrative costs could be financed, at least in part, with monies raised under state law, so long as the party committees maintained separate bank accounts for their federal and nonfederal monies.[15] This decision was especially important because state laws allow contributions in amounts and from sources that are prohibited under the FECA. For example, many states—in fact, most states at the time of the ruling—allow parties to accept money from corporations and labor unions or have no limits on the amount a donor can contribute to a political party. Accordingly, the FEC decision gave the national party committees access to the types of contribution that were banned by the FECA. Suddenly, party committees once again could accept unlimited contributions from individuals, groups, or corporations and labor unions, so long as they deposited these gifts in a segregated bank account.

Thus was born the notion of "hard" and "soft" money. "Hard money" is the colloquial term used to describe the funds raised by party committees that are subject to federal contribution limits. Presumably, this term is applied to federally regulated contributions because they are harder to raise than "soft money" funds, which is the colloquial term used to describe the unregulated contributions parties raise to pay for their activities that are not related to federal elections.

Throughout the 1980s and early 1990s, party organizations expanded their use of soft money to finance a wide range of party costs and activities. National party committees, including the national Senate and House campaign committees in both major parties, began to finance a share of their administrative expenses, staff salaries, fundraising costs, party-building efforts, and general advertising with soft money. In practice, they were free to spend unlimited amounts of money from unlimited sources, so long as they abided by the technical legalities of the FEC regulations. About the only restraint on soft money spending is the prohibition against using these funds directly to help federal candidates; in other words, soft money cannot be used to make contributions to federal candidates, finance coordinated spending, or pay for independent expenditures.

ISSUE ADVOCACY

The other major area of campaign finance that is not controlled by federal law is the type of political communication known as "issue advocacy." As noted previously, in ruling on the constitutionality of campaign finance laws, courts have distinguished speech that expressly advocates the election or defeat of a candidate from other types of political speech. According to the *Buckley* decision, Congress may regulate express advocacy, but it may not regulate communications that do not meet this standard, such as communications that advocate issues, present information about issues, or, most important, provide background information about candidates. This latter category of communications—information about candidates, information about issues, and advocacy of particular issues or policies—is commonly known as "issue advocacy."

The problem that courts have had to face is the central question of how to separate express advocacy from issue advocacy. After all, voters often decide to support candidates based on what they know about them, or on their knowledge of the issues candidates advocate or the specific policies they have supported. Issue advocacy can therefore influence the outcome of federal elections, just as express advocacy can.

In resolving this issue, courts have sought a "bright line" that can be used to distinguish express advocacy from issue advocacy, so that those engaging in political speech are aware of the law and the applicability of federal regulations, and so that any potential First Amendment problems are clearly avoided. Most courts have therefore embraced the "magic words" test that was suggested by the Supreme Court in *Buckley*. Under these rulings, a message or advertisement is not considered to be express advocacy if it does not contain such words as "vote for," "elect," "defeat," "support," or "Candidate X for Congress."[16]

So, any communications or advertisements that avoid the words used to signal express advocacy are considered issue advocacy under the law. These communications therefore fall outside of the scope of federal regulation. They can be financed with unlimited contributions from any source, including corporate and labor union treasury funds. Moreover, they are not subject to federal disclosure requirements, so the organizations or individuals sponsoring such ads do not have to report to the FEC the source of their funds, the amounts being raised or spent, or where the money is being spent.

Given the lack of restrictions on soft money and issue advocacy, it is not surprising that these forms of finance are growing rapidly. Nor is it surprising that they have become the most controversial aspects of the campaign finance system. Most advocates of change condemn these practices and call for their reform, rightfully contending that they have undermined the intent of the

FECA and rendered most of its provisions meaningless. But soft money and issue advocacy are not the only issues in the current campaign finance reform debate. Many other concerns have been raised by developments within the regulated system. It is therefore appropriate to review these issues before considering the consequences of such unregulated activities as soft money and issue advocacy.

3

THE COSTS OF CAMPAIGNING

At the center of the campaign finance debate are the issue of rising costs and the basic question: Is campaign spending too high? Many advocates of reform claim that campaign spending is out of control and that the steep increase in expenditures that has taken place in recent decades demonstrates the failure of the current system. According to this view, rising campaign expenses have made it necessary for candidates to spend more and more time raising money and have priced out of the process prospective candidates who feel they cannot raise the funds needed to wage a viable campaign. Escalating costs thus have increased the emphasis candidates place on fundraising and, consequently, increased the potential influence of money in the political process.

Others argue that election spending is not exorbitant given the size and diversity of our nation and the number of elective offices to be filled in federal, state, and local governments. Candidates need to communicate with large electorates, which means that they must often rely on television and radio advertising to make their views known. Such broad-based communication is costly but essential to the creation of an informed electorate. Some advocates therefore encourage additional spending in order to promote political discourse and give greater prominence to election campaigns amidst the deluge of competing messages and information available to the public in our society.

As with many types of spending, this debate goes on in part because there is no universally accepted criterion for judging campaign expenditures. It is therefore difficult to determine when political spending should be considered excessive or whether particular expenditures are unjustified. Nor is it easy to decide how much spending is enough in any particular contest, given the highly differentiated character of elections throughout the nation. What is generally accepted is the fact that campaign spending has grown at a rapid rate, and that the costs of running for office are likely to continue to rise in the future.

HOW MUCH DO WE SPEND ON POLITICAL CAMPAIGNS?

During the 1996 election cycle, candidates, political committees, and other organizations and individuals spent an estimated $4 billion on political campaigns.[1] This spending covered not only the races for the White House and seats in Congress but also contests for state and local offices, efforts by political parties and other organizations to register and turn out voters, the costs incurred by political party organizations at all levels of government, and the numerous political committees sponsored by interest groups and other associations.

This $4 billion total represents an increase of almost 25 percent over the amount spent in 1992. The 1996 election thus continued a decades-long trend of spiraling campaign costs. Since 1972, the amount spent on political campaigns has grown from an estimated $425 million to $4 billion, an increase of close to 850 percent (see Table 3.1).[2] Even when adjusted for inflation, the rise in spending is significant. For example, from 1976 to 1996, the consumer price index rose by slightly more than 300 percent, while political spending rose more than 700 percent.

This growth in campaign spending has been led by the increasing sums spent on campaigns for federal office. Over the past two decades, the total amount spent by candidates seeking a seat in the House or Senate rose from $115.5 million in 1976 to $735.8 million in 1998. In the presidential race, spending by candidates seeking the major party nominations grew from a total of $114 million in 1976 to $348 million in 1996.[3] Average House expenditures during this period rose from $73,000 to $493,000, while the average Senate campaign cost grew from $595,000 to $3.3 million. For winning candidates, the costs were even higher. The average amount spent by House winners in 1998 was about $660,000, while Senate winners spent an average of $4.6 million.[4] Even when controlled for inflation, spending levels in congressional contests have more than doubled since 1976.[5]

Moreover, these figures for candidate spending do not truly reflect the actual amounts spent on federal campaigns since they do not include the

TABLE 3.1
TOTAL POLITICAL SPENDING, 1972–96 ($ MILLIONS)

Election Year	Total
1972	425
1976	540
1980	1,200
1984	1,800
1988	2,700
1992	3,220
1996	4,000

Source: Figures for 1972–92 are taken from Herbert Alexander and Anthony Corrado, *Financing the 1992 Election* (Armonk, N.Y.: M. E. Sharpe, 1995), p. 6. The figure for 1996 is based on data prepared by the Citizens' Research Foundation.

amounts spent by political parties to assist their candidates and to stage national party conventions or the amounts spent by political committees or other individuals independent of the candidates. If such spending is included in the totals, the amounts expended rise significantly. For example, Herbert Alexander of the Citizens' Research Foundation has estimated that when monies from all sources are considered, including the candidates, party committees, and outside groups, the actual amount spent electing a president has grown from $160 million in 1976 to $700 million in 1996.[6]

While spending at the federal level has grown, it has not been a steady increase. For example, a 1997 study of Federal Election Commission (FEC) campaign finance data by the Cato Institute found that the 1982 and 1986 federal elections were more expensive than the 1994 elections, when spending is adjusted for inflation.[7] In 1990, spending in congressional races declined slightly as compared to 1988, and in 1998, spending was down as compared to the total achieved two years earlier. The overall trend, however, is clearly upward, and the occasional declines do not suggest that this pattern will change anytime soon (see Table 3.2, page 30).

In 1998, for example, the amount spent by House and Senate candidates declined slightly, totaling $735.8 million, as compared to $759.1 million in 1996. Spending in Senate races was slightly higher than in 1996 ($287.5 million versus $286.6 million), but House expenditures declined from $472.5 million in 1996 to $448.3 million. This decline was due largely to a decline in competition rather than any change in the costs of elections or in the attitudes

TABLE 3.2
CONGRESSIONAL CAMPAIGN SPENDING,
1976–98 ($ MILLIONS)

Election Year	Senate	House	Total
1976	44.0	71.5	115.5
1978	85.2	109.7	194.8
1980	102.9	136.0	239.0
1982	138.4	204.0	342.4
1984	170.5	203.6	374.1
1986	211.6	239.3	450.9
1988	201.2	256.5	457.7
1990	180.4	265.8	446.3
1992	271.6	406.7	678.3
1994	318.4	405.6	724.0
1996	286.6	472.5	759.1
1998	287.5	448.3	735.8

Source: Based on data reported by the Federal Election Commission.

of candidates toward campaign spending. In 1998, a total of 2,100 candidates sought a seat in Congress, as opposed to 2,605 candidates two years earlier.[8] More important, there were fewer open-seat races for the House than in any election since 1990, and these races tend to be more expensive owing to the high level of competition that typically occurs in such contests. In the other contests, many incumbents faced opponents who were severely underfunded, which resulted in a lower level of challenger spending than in previous elections. In fact, all of the decline in House spending in 1998 can be attributed to the decline in challenger spending.

While the amounts spent by political candidates and committees are substantial, the sums remain relatively low when compared with other types of spending. In 1988 and 1992, for example, the total election expenses of all candidates and political committees was less than the amount spent by the nation's two leading commercial advertisers, Proctor and Gamble and Philip Morris, in promoting their products.[9] And even a well-financed congressional candidate, one who spends up to $500,000 in a campaign, is spending less than $1.50 per person to reach those individuals of voting age in the average congressional district.

Why Are Costs Increasing?

No one factor can explain the growth that has taken place in the cost of campaigns. Changes in the size of electoral districts, innovations in campaign strategies, new technologies, shifting levels of competition, and the behavior of candidates and political groups all contribute to the changes that have taken place in recent decades. Among these various explanations, the most commonly cited factor is the growth in spending on media advertising, particularly television and radio advertising.

Television advertising has become an increasingly prominent component of political campaigns since the 1960s. National and statewide candidates rely on television to communicate their views to the large electorates they hope to represent. Paid advertising has become the preferred method of communication for those seeking federal and statewide office because it allows a candidate to speak directly to voters and to control the content of the message being distributed.

The use of television advertising has had a major effect on the amounts expended in federal campaigns. The Television Bureau of Advertising estimates that primary and general election candidates for federal, state, and local offices spent a total of $50.8 million on television advertising in 1976. By 1996, candidate spending on television had reached $400 million (see Table 3.3).[10] Even when adjusted for inflation, this represents a real increase of more than 200 percent over the past five presidential election cycles.

As might be expected, television advertising has had the greatest effect on spending in presidential races, where candidates must communicate with a

TABLE 3.3
COST OF POLITICAL BROADCAST ADVERTISING, 1976–96

Election Year	Total ($)
1976	50,842,200
1980	90,570,000
1984	153,824,000
1988	227,900,200
1992	299,623,400
1996	400,485,900

Source: Joseph E. Cantor, Denis Steven Rutkus, and Kevin B. Greely, *Free and Reduced-Rate Television Time for Political Candidates* (Washington, D.C.: Congressional Research Service, 1997), p. 5.

national electorate. In 1996, for example, President Bill Clinton allocated 52 percent ($59.1 million) of his campaign expenditures to media advertising, while his opponent, Senator Robert Dole, devoted 46 percent ($53.9 million) to such advertising. In the general election campaign alone, both candidates spent more than 60 percent of their campaign funds on advertising, with Clinton devoting 63 percent of his budget to this cost and Dole 61 percent of his.[11]

Broadcast advertising represents a smaller share of the budget in congressional campaigns, but it is still a major expense in most of these races, especially in Senate contests. According to recent studies based on detailed examinations of Federal Election Commission disclosure reports, less than half of the monies spent by U.S. Senate and House candidates are devoted to electronic media advertising. Major party Senate candidates in 1992 spent 42 percent of their funds ($91.8 million) on electronic media advertising, including payments to media consultants, direct radio and television airtime purchases, and advertising production costs. Major party House candidates that year spent 27 percent of their monies ($88.2 million) on electronic advertising. House candidates make less use of television and radio advertising than do other federal candidates because it is not a cost-effective means of campaigning in many districts, especially those in major metropolitan areas, where media markets are much larger than a single House district. In fact, more than one-fourth of the House incumbents seeking reelection in 1990 spent no money at all on broadcast advertising. These candidates either could not afford media advertising or made greater use of more targeted communications, such as direct mail. Similar spending patterns characterized Senate and House races in 1994.[12]

Another major expense in most federal campaigns is the cost of raising money. As expenditures have risen, candidates have had to devote large sums to fundraising. The costs vary with the office being sought, the financial needs of a campaign, and the fundraising methods used. In general, fundraising expenses represent 10 to 20 percent of the costs of a federal campaign, with the average higher for incumbents (who typically raise more money) than for challengers.[13]

The rising cost of other campaign staples also has contributed to the growth in spending. Such basic expenses as postage, mail, and travel have increased at rates greater than inflation, driving up the actual cost of campaigns. For example, between 1976 and 1980, the consumer price index rose about 40 percent, while the cost of mass mailings rose by 50 percent and air travel by 300 percent. In addition, modern campaigns rely on an array of consultants and sophisticated new technologies, including polling, computerized direct mail, and teleconferencing services, all of which add to the cost of campaigns. The result, as FEC commissioner Lee Ann Elliott observed in 1992, is that "campaign costs don't go up at market basket inflation; instead of going up about four or five percent every year, they go up ten, twelve, fifteen percent every year."[14]

Candidate behavior also produces greater spending. Most candidates fear being outspent by an opponent and worry about not spending enough on a campaign. Since no politician can know with certainty which forms of spending are most effective in garnering support, candidates tend to spend as much as they can raise, due to their fear of being outspent by an opponent or of failing to spend enough in a particular area that may prove important to an election's outcome.

The changing patterns of competition also encourage increased candidate spending. The rise of the Republican Party in the South and the shifting partisan majorities in Congress over the past decade have produced more competitive and fiercely fought contests. In the early 1990s, many incumbents chose not to seek reelection because of reapportionment and redistricting or the popular revolt against incumbency that characterized some areas of the nation or personal concerns. Consequently, the number of open seats, which are usually the most hotly contested because of the lack of an incumbent, rose from 60 in 1990 to 144 in 1992. The growth in the number of first-term members of Congress led to a further increase in competition, since most observers consider incumbents to be most vulnerable in their first bid for reelection. Even greater levels of competition characterized the elections conducted after 1994, when majority control of the House shifted to the Republican party. Since then, the two major parties have battled for control of the legislature, with the Republican margin declining in each of the past two elections. As a result, only six seats now determine the House majority. The 2000 election is therefore likely to be the most fiercely contested race in recent years, since the House majority, as well as the White House, are clearly up for grabs.

The heightened level of competition has encouraged candidates to raise and spend money with great zeal and spurred the party organizations to devote increasingly large sums to their efforts to assist their candidates for federal office. Total spending in congressional races rose from about $446 million in 1990 to $680 million in 1992 and $765 million in 1996. Party spending in congressional elections also rose from about $24 million in 1990 (including party contributions to candidates and any coordinated spending) to approximately $56 million in 1996.[15] This dramatic growth in overall expenditures suggests the extent to which electoral competition is a determinant of campaign spending.

Much of this spending tends to be concentrated in marginal House districts and states with Senate races where the outcome of the election is uncertain. These districts and states represent opportunities for one party or another, or one interest or another, to gain support in Congress, and they therefore tend to attract the most financial support and the most voter interest. In these districts, House races costing $500,000 to $1 million or more are increasingly common. They also tend to be the focus of party spending. But such districts constitute a minority—in recent years less than a quarter—of the 435 congressional seats up for election every two years. So the increase in costs is particularly acute for candidates in these contests, while candidates in many other districts spend significantly less because they either face little competition or find it difficult to raise even the minimal amount needed to wage a viable campaign. These variances should be kept in mind when considering the aggregate spending trends that have come to characterize federal elections.

WHY ARE RISING COSTS A PROBLEM?

While there are some who are not concerned about rising campaign costs and even advocate further spending as a means of promoting the amount of political speech in the system and the level of public participation in the financing of campaigns, most advocates of campaign reform argue that the dramatic increase in the cost of campaigning is one of the clearest signs of the declining health of our political system.

As costs rise, the sums needed to mount a viable campaign increase, which means that fundraising becomes more important. Candidates must develop a broad base of donors and be willing to devote substantial amounts of time to fundraising if they hope to be competitive in a typical congressional race. This increased emphasis on fundraising heightens the concerns about the influence of money in the political process and the effect of contributions on candidate behavior. Further, many individuals lack the resources and personal contacts needed to generate the hundreds of thousands of dollars now required for most House races. These potential candidates are thus effectively priced out of the market, which reduces the pool of citizens capable of mounting bids for our nation's highest offices and significantly reduces the choices available to the electorate.

The emphasis on fundraising also influences the kind of candidates recruited by party committees. Most of the candidates in the 1996 House races were formerly in business or banking, law, or other white-collar professions.[16] Such candidates have the contacts and financial experience and, in some cases, the personal wealth needed to generate the sums of money necessary in modern campaigns. Thus, in 1996, the Democrats recruited corporate executives to be challengers for Senate seats since such candidates had the financial background and probusiness philosophies that some party leaders believed were valuable assets in high-cost Senate campaigns.[17]

   Even those incumbents who have well-established fundraising operations must spend substantial amounts of time raising money to meet the anticipated costs of their next campaign. Senator Barbara Boxer, a Democrat from California, has summarized the problem legislators face as follows: "Today, a senate candidate in California can expect to have to raise up to $10,000 per day, including Saturday and Sunday, 365 days a year, for six full years. That is too much time away from work, too much time away from doing the kinds of things that we want to do [in Congress], making life better for people."[18] Similarly, former senator Nancy Kassebaum, a Republican from Kansas, while still serving in the Senate, observed that "we are forced to raise money all the time. . . . I worry about the energy it takes. [Senators are] out there raising money all the time. We don't sit down and talk to each other very much anymore. We don't have time."[19]

   These views are not unique. A wide array of former legislators have complained about the amount of time they had to spend raising money, and a number of them have cited "the money chase" as a factor in their decisions to leave Congress.[20] Part of the reason why legislators must spend an increasing amount of time raising funds is that the contribution limits have not kept pace with inflation. The value of a contribution, the amount of services it can purchase, has diminished significantly since 1974. By 1998, the $1,000 donation could purchase less than $350 in services. Candidates therefore have to raise close to three times as much as their counterparts did twenty years ago just to gain the same value. And the real cost of campaigns has outpaced inflation during this period.

4

SOURCES OF FUNDING

The money for federal campaigns essentially comes from four sources: individuals, PACs, party funds, and candidates' personal resources. Presidential candidates also can qualify for public funding. Of these, donations from individuals are the largest source of funds. In 1996, more than 1.2 million individual contributions of $200 or more were received by federal candidates and party committees, in addition to millions of additional small contributions of less than $200. PACs, which like party committees aggregate the contributions of millions of small donors, made another 230,000 contributions to federal candidates and party committees.[1] The role of these various donors in the financing of federal political activity is best discerned by examining the sources of all the monies in the federal system, as well as the funding of different types of candidates.

After the 1996 election, the Center for Responsive Politics conducted an analysis of the sources of funding in federal elections. The findings offer a basic overview of campaign financing at the federal level. According to this study, individual contributors provided more than 60 percent ($1.3 billion) of the $2.1 billion raised by all federal candidates, PACs, and party committees for the 1996 elections. Small contributors of less than $200 gave a total of $734 million, while individual donors of $200 or more gave a total of $597 million. Individual donors were the most important source of funding for candidates, parties, and PACs. PACs donated $243 million in 1996, public financing provided $211 million, and candidates spent $161 million of their own money. The remaining $200 million came from miscellaneous sources, primarily bank loans and the interest earned on campaign accounts.[2] These figures do not include the $262 million in unlimited soft money contributions raised by party committees. Since these contributions are not subject to FECA limits and cannot be used to provide direct assistance to federal candidates, they will be considered separately in a later section.

Regardless of the office being sought, most of the money received by federal candidates comes from the voluntary contributions of individual donors. On average, individual contributions are the source of slightly less than half of the total funding received by House candidates and more than 50 percent of the monies raised in Senate campaigns. PACs are the next-largest source, providing from 35 to 40 percent of the monies in House races and approximately 18 to 20 percent of the funds in Senate races. Party committees provide about 5 percent of the money in House races and a little less than 10 percent of the revenue in Senate races, while candidates' personal contributions account for 5 to 9 percent of the money in House campaigns and 5 to 10 percent of the money in Senate contests.[3]

In presidential races, the pattern is very different, largely due to the option of public funding. In primary elections from 1976 through 1996, most of the money raised by presidential contenders came from individual donors and the public monies generated by small individual donations. On average, candidates for the presidential nomination who participate in the public funding program raise more than 90 percent of their total funds from individuals and public funding, with individual donations constituting more than 60 percent of total receipts and public matching funds about a third. As these statistics suggest, PACs have not been an important source of revenue in presidential campaigns. Even presidential aspirants who specifically target PAC donations rarely receive more than 5 percent of their total primary funds from this source. Presidential candidates do not have a strong incentive to pursue PAC money because PAC gifts are not eligible for public matching funds. In addition, most PACs choose to concentrate their resources on congressional campaigns, and some have a policy of not participating in presidential races.[4] As a result, PAC financing has not been a source of major controversy at the presidential level.

WHAT IS THE ROLE OF INDIVIDUAL DONORS IN THE FINANCING OF CAMPAIGNS?

In 1972, approximately 1,200 individuals gave a total of $51 million to the presidential campaigns alone, in contributions of $10,000 or more.[5] One of the objectives of the FECA was to eliminate these large individual gifts and to replace them with small contributions from a broad base of individual donors. To a large degree, this purpose has been achieved. Each year, hundreds of thousands of individuals contribute to federal campaigns and party committees. In the 1996 elections alone, some 630,000 individuals gave $200 or more to a federal candidate or party committee, including more than 230,000 who each gave at least $1,000.[6] And these figures do not include the monies individuals contributed to PACs or party soft money accounts.

Most of the money in federal elections thus comes from a broad base of individual donors. But, even though hundreds of thousands of citizens now participate financially in federal elections, those who choose to make a contribution represent a relatively small share of the electorate. While it is impossible to determine exactly how many persons give to federal candidates (because federal law does not require itemized disclosure of contributors of less than $200), survey research indicates that only about one out of every twenty Americans directly contributes money to a candidate or political party. About 4 percent of the electorate say they give money to a political party, while about 6 percent give to political candidates, and this includes elections at all levels of government. These percentages have remained stable since 1980 but represent a decline since the 1960s, when 10 to 12 percent of the adult population reported contribution activity.[7] Those who do contribute tend to be better educated, more financially secure, and more politically active members of the electorate.

An even smaller share of the public—less than one-tenth of 1 percent of the population—gives $1,000 or more to federal candidates or political parties. Yet this relatively small group, which includes at least 275 individuals who actually exceeded the maximum legal individual contribution of $25,000 in 1996, provides a sizable share of the revenue in the federal system. In 1996, these $1,000 donors contributed a total of $477 million, or approximately 23 percent of all the monies contributed to parties and candidates in federal elections.[8]

In assessing these levels of participation, it is important to note that the relatively low level of financial participation by members of the electorate may be due in part to the relatively small number of citizens who are asked to contribute. A recent study indicates that only about 22 percent of the electorate are ever asked to make a contribution to a political campaign. Of those who are asked, about 27 percent do give.[9] So one major reason why such a small share of the public makes political contributions is that only a small share is asked to give, and thus one way to increase the number who participate in the financing of elections may be to ask more people to contribute.

More disconcerting than the relatively small pool of donors is the diminishing role of the small donor in the financing of federal campaigns. As the cost of these contests has increased, most candidates have emphasized the solicitation of larger amounts from donors since it is a more efficient means of garnering the large sums needed to finance a viable campaign, requiring less expensive and time-consuming approaches than direct mail and telemarketing, which are the usual way to reach small donors.

Consequently, in recent elections, major party congressional candidates have raised a growing share of the money they solicit from individuals in contributions of $500 or more (see Table 4.1). In 1984, Senate candidates in all elections (primary, general, and runoff elections) raised about 41 percent of their total individual contributions in donations of $500 or more. By 1998, this proportion had grown to 63 percent. During this same period, the large-donor share of the individual contributions received by House candidates rose from 34 percent to 53 percent.[10]

TABLE 4.1
CONTRIBUTORS OF $500 OR MORE AS A PERCENTAGE
OF INDIVIDUAL CONTRIBUTIONS, 1984–98

Election Year	Senate	House	President
1984	40.9	34.2	41.1
1988	54.3	41.7	51.1
1992	53.1	45.8	45.4
1994	54.4	49.0	n/a
1996	60.2	50.6	42.1
1998	63.0	53.0	n/a

Source: Based on data reported by the Federal Election Commission.

Large individual gifts have become an important source of revenue for both incumbents and challengers. In 1998, for example, Senate incumbents raised almost 75 percent of the total received from individuals in contributions of $500 or more. Senate challengers received slightly more than 60 percent of their total from this source. In House races, these large donations made up almost 54 percent of the individual receipts of incumbents and more than 48 percent of the total amount individuals gave to challengers.

This growth in large-donor funding is not as pronounced in the presidential race, mainly because the presidential public funding program provides contenders with an incentive to seek smaller donations. Yet even in this case, the rise in the number of large donors and amounts raised from these gifts is significant. For example, in 1984 the major party presidential challengers received 41 percent of their total individual receipts from contributions of $500 or more. In

1996, the candidates received 42 percent of their individual monies from such contributions. The amounts received, however, differed greatly. In 1984, the candidates raised almost 58,000 contributions of $500 or more, for a total of about $48.8 million. In 1996, the candidates raised more than 91,000 such gifts, for a total of about $81.4 million. Conversely, the portion of congressional candidate funding derived from contributions of less than $200 is declining. Although comparable data are not available for elections prior to 1992, the change since 1992 is noteworthy. In that year, Senate candidates raised 36 percent of their individual funding, $67.1 million, from small contributions. By 1998, the share had dropped to 29 percent, or a total of $47.6 million. In House races, the share of funding from small individual donors has slipped from about 39 percent in 1992 to 33 percent in 1998. The total amount raised from small donors has increased, however, from $78 million in 1992 to more than $84 million in 1998, or a 10 percent rise over the past four elections. But this growth in small gifts has been outweighed by the greater increase in revenues from large gifts.

Furthermore, these data understate the role of large donors in congressional campaigns, or overstate the role of small donors, since they are based on individual contributions, not the aggregate amount given by an individual contributor. It can be safely assumed that some of these donors made more than one contribution to a candidate and thus gave more than $500. Similarly, some multiple donors certainly made contributions totaling more than $200 that are not reflected in the small-donor estimates. The overall pattern, however, is clear: candidates are turning to larger contributors when seeking the monies needed to finance their campaigns.

The disproportionate role of large donors in the financing of congressional campaigns has led some observers to decry the potential influence of these donors and the access or special considerations they may receive as a result of their contributions. They argue further that such differences in financial participation violate the principle of political equality since some individuals are able to give $1,000 or more to a candidate, while others give only small amounts or cannot afford to contribute at all. They would prefer financial participation to be more equitable; just as individuals have an equal ability to vote, so too should they have an equal ability to participate in other ways. They therefore tend to support lower contribution limits or public financing as a means of improving the equity in the system.[11]

Others contend that a substantial amount of equality already has been achieved as a result of the $1,000 contribution limit. They further note that the role of individual contributions is diminished by the current law since contributions are not adjusted to account for inflation. If adjusted, the individual limit would currently be more than $3,000 per election, which would allow individuals to play an even greater role in the financing of campaigns.

WHAT IS THE ROLE OF PACs IN THE FINANCING OF ELECTIONS?

One of the most prominent changes to take place in the federal campaign finance system since the adoption of the reforms of the 1970s is the emergence of PACs as a major source of funding in congressional elections (see Table 4.2). In the two decades since the FECA was adopted, the number of PACs has grown from approximately 600 in 1974 to more than 4,600 in 1998. The greatest growth has come in the number of PACs affiliated with corporations, which rose from 89 in 1974 to almost 1,800 in 1998, and in the number of PACs organized by ideological groups, which increased from less than 200 in 1978 to approximately 1,400 in 1998. (PACs in the latter group are called "non-connected" PACs by the FEC because they are not connected to a corporation or labor union.) The number of trade association PACs rose from 453 in 1978 to 900 in 1998, while PACs organized by labor unions grew from slightly more than 200 in 1974 to 348 in 1998.

TABLE 4.2
GROWTH OF PACs, 1974–98

Election Year	Corporate	Trade Association	Labor	Non-connected	Other
1974	89	318[a]	201	—	—
1976	433	489[a]	224	—	—
1978	785	453	217	162	36
1980	1,206	576	297	374	98
1982	1,469	649	380	723	150
1984	1,682	698	394	1,053	182
1986	1,744	745	384	1,077	207
1988	1,816	786	354	1,115	197
1990	1,795	774	346	1,062	195
1992	1,735	770	347	1,145	198
1994	1,660	792	333	980	189
1996	1,642	838	332	1,103	164
1998	1,778	900	348	1,399	173

[a] These figures represent all other PACs for 1974–76.
Source: Based on data reported by the Federal Election Commission.

While PACs are commonly cast as single-interest organizations or "special interests," they collectively represent thousands of different groups and tens of thousands of individual donors. All PAC monies contributed to candidates must come from voluntary contributions made to the PAC, which are limited under federal law. Advocates of these organizations therefore observe that PACs provide small donors with a means of participating in a broader group that represents their concerns.

The amount of money PACs have donated to House and Senate candidates has increased significantly, rising from about $34 million in 1978 to about $206 million in 1998 (see Table 4.3). A substantial share of this funding comes from PACs associated with corporations. In all, corporate PACs donated more than $76 million to federal candidates in 1998 (including contributions made to senators not seeking election in 1998), as compared to almost $62 million by trade association PACs, $44 million by labor PACs, and $28 million by non-connected PACs.[12] Corporate PACs thus donated the largest sum in 1998, but the average amount contributed by each of these was $42,800, as compared to an average of approximately $126,000 by labor PACs and $20,000 by non-connected PACs.

TABLE 4.3
PAC CONTRIBUTIONS TO CONGRESSIONAL CANDIDATES, 1978–98 ($ MILLIONS)

Election Year	Senate	House	Total
1978	24.4	9.7	34.1
1980	37.9	17.3	55.2
1982	61.1	22.5	83.6
1984	75.6	29.7	105.3
1986	87.4	45.3	132.7
1988	102.2	45.7	147.9
1990	108.5	41.2	149.7
1992	127.4	51.2	178.6
1994	132.1	46.7	178.8
1996	155.8	45.6	201.4
1998	158.5	48.1	206.6

Source: Based on data reported by the Federal Election Commission.

Most of the contributions made by PACs go to incumbents. PACs tend to be pragmatic actors in the political process, supporting those candidates who share their views and often trying to maximize the value of their donations by focusing their resources on those candidates with a good prospect of winning. Overall, approximately 70 percent of the monies contributed by PACs go to incumbents, and about 10 to 15 percent to those challenging incumbents. The other 15 to 18 percent of these donations are made to candidates involved in open-seat races.[13] For example, in 1998, about 75 percent of the $206 million donated by PACs went to incumbents. Senate incumbents received $34.3 million from PACs, a total five times greater than the $6.5 million given to challengers. In House races, incumbents received $123.9 million, as compared to only $14.8 million given to challengers. PACs alone were thus responsible for providing incumbents with a more than $136 million advantage over their opponents.[14]

PACs divided their funding fairly evenly between Republican and Democratic incumbents, although a majority of the funds went to Republicans, who controlled both houses of Congress. Overall, PACs gave almost $83 million to Republican officeholders, as compared to $75 million to Democrats. The 1998 election thus continued the long-standing trend of more PAC money being given to members of the majority party. The fourteen Republicans seeking reelection to the Senate raised $18.7 million from PACs, or an average of $1.3 million each, while the fifteen Democrats raised $15.6 million, or an average of slightly more than $1 million. In the House races, the 212 Republicans seeking reelection received $64.2 million, while the 194 Democratic incumbents received $59.7 million each. While the overall amount received by Republicans was greater, Democratic members actually received a slightly larger amount on average, $307,700, as compared to $302,800 for the Republicans.

In addition to favoring incumbents, the patterns of giving by PACs also demonstrate some other general tendencies. Corporate PACs tend to be the most pragmatic, primarily supporting incumbents. Non-connected PACs tend to focus their donations on candidates who share their particular ideological or policy preferences, regardless of incumbency status. Labor PACs focus most of their donations on candidates closely allied with the Democratic party.[15]

These general observations, however, mask the great diversity in resources that characterized different PACs. PACs vary greatly in the extent to which they participate in the financing of political campaigns. As noted in Table 4.4,[16] more than one out of three PACs active in the 1998 election cycle contributed no monies to federal candidates. Another 20 percent contributed a total of $5,000 or less. So more than half (55 percent) of the PACs active in the 1998 elections made total contributions, including all donations made to federal candidates, of $5,000 or less. In fact, less than 4 percent of the active

PACs made contributions that totaled $250,000 or more. This relatively small group of committees was responsible for more than $171 million in contributions, or 56 percent of all the monies donated by PACs in 1997 and 1998. These data, which are comparable to the patterns of 1992 and 1996,[17] suggest that the perceived problems with PACs are not as extensive as many reformers contend and that, at best, any concerns about the role of PACs are concerns associated with a relatively small number of committees.

TABLE 4.4
PACs CLASSIFIED BY THE SIZE OF THEIR TOTAL CONTRIBUTIONS, 1997–98

Amount of PACs' Total Contributions ($ Millions)	Number of PACs	Percentage of all PACs	Total Contributions ($ Millions)	Percentage of all PAC Spending
None	1,620	35.2	0.0	0.0
Less than 5	927	20.2	1.9	0.9
5–50	1,257	27.3	25.0	11.6
50–100	330	7.2	23.5	10.9
100–250	285	6.2	44.2	20.4
250–500	94	2.0	33.2	15.3
500–1,000	51	1.1	35.7	16.5
More than 1,000	34	0.7	52.6	24.3
Total	4,598	100	216.1	100

Note: Percentages may not total 100 percent due to rounding.
Source: Based on data through November 23, 1998, reported by the Federal Election Commission. Figures include all contributions made during the two-year cycle.

WHY ARE PACs SO CONTROVERSIAL?

Although the proportion of PACs that contribute significant sums to federal candidates is relatively small, these committees have provoked a substantial amount of controversy. Some advocates of reform, led by Common Cause and other public interest groups, argue that these organizations distort the electoral process and allow "special interests" unduly to influence public policy. Numerous reports have documented a relationship between PAC contributions and legislative actions, whether it be decisions made in committee or votes taken on the floor of the House or Senate. Studies of tobacco policy, agricultural subsidies, and defense procurement contracts, among others, have demonstrated a strong relationship between the votes cast by legislators and PAC contributions. In general, these studies find that most of the legislators who receive money from the PACs interested in these policies support the positions these PACs advocate.[18]

Similarly, the recent patterns in PAC giving suggest that many of these committees use their contributions to gain access or stay in favor with legislators. For example, when the Democrats controlled Congress, business PACs gave the majority of their contributions to Democrats. In 1992, Democrats received about 53 percent of business PAC dollars; in 1994, about 51 percent. But these committees shifted their strategy dramatically after the Republicans gained control of Congress in 1995. Beginning immediately after election day in 1994, business PACs gave the vast majority of their money to Republicans, eventually donating 70 percent of their monies to Republicans.[19] Recent research on the timing of PAC donations also suggests that PACs give in order to influence legislative voting. This research shows that PAC contributions increase in the weeks surrounding legislative action of importance to PACs and that PACs tend to target legislators who are "on the fence" on a particular issue in an effort to secure their support.[20]

While there is a substantial amount of evidence that suggests that PACs do gain undue policy influence as a result of their donations, scholarly studies of PAC behavior largely have failed to document this influence. Most of these studies have found that PAC contributions do not have a major effect on legislative voting behavior. Voting by members of Congress is best explained by a member's ideology, party affiliation, and constituency interests; it is not a result of the sources of campaign money.

However, it may be that these studies, because they primarily look at congressional voting, underestimate the effect of contributions. Compared to other legislative acts, votes are the most public and easy to analyze. Legislators can expect that their votes will be scrutinized closely, so it is here that an interest group is likely to have the least influence. But a very small proportion of the bills submitted to Congress ever come to a vote; only about 15 to 20 percent of the bills submitted are ever referred to committee, and only about 4 percent become law—and many of these are noncontroversial resolutions. The influence of PACs therefore may be found not in the votes that actually occur but rather in the actions that are not taken by Congress—the decisions to kill a proposal by not referring it to a committee, or not scheduling it for hearings, or not calling it up for a vote.[21]

What Is the Role of Personal Wealth in Federal Campaigns?

Most of the money contributed by individuals and PACs goes to incumbents. Challengers are therefore almost always at a financial disadvantage, and most challengers are outspent by significant margins. In recent elections, an increasing number of challengers have tried to overcome this financial problem by dipping into their own pockets and either directly contributing money to their campaigns or making a loan to their campaigns. As a result, one of the most noteworthy trends in recent elections is the significant rise in the number of self-financed candidates.

In 1996, fifty-four Senate candidates and ninety-one House candidates each put $100,000 or more of their own money into their campaigns, either through direct contributions or loans.[22] (The difference between a contribution and a loan is that a loan can be repaid from monies raised by the candidate, particularly monies raised after a candidate has won.) In the 1998 general election campaigns, Senate candidates gave about $28.4 million to their own campaigns, and their House counterparts contributed close to $25.4 million.

These amounts represent a substantial increase as compared to earlier elections. In 1988, for example, Senate candidates used $9.7 million of their own funds, while House candidates gave themselves $12.5 million. In percentage terms, the share of total Senate general election campaign receipts that came from personal funds rose from 5.4 percent in 1988 to 11.5 percent in 1998. In House races, the percentage of all monies from personal funds rose from 5.2 percent in 1988 to 6.0 percent in 1998.[23]

And 1998 was not a record-breaking year. In 1994, a year when control of both the House and Senate were hotly contested, Senate candidates spent $53.7 million out of their own pockets, and their House counterparts spent $26.6 million, for a total of about $80 million in personal money. In the Senate races alone, about one out of every five dollars raised in 1994 came from the bank accounts of the candidates themselves. This unusually large proportion of personal money was primarily due to the extraordinary sums donated to their own campaigns by Michael Huffington of California ($27.8 million), Herb Kohl of Wisconsin ($6.5 million), and Bill Frist of Tennessee ($3.7 million).[24]

It is unlikely, however, that 1994 will remain the high-water mark for personal spending very long. Given the financial patterns exhibited early in the 2000 election cycle, a new high is likely to be achieved in this year. As of March 2000, candidates for House and Senate seats already had contributed or loaned more than $53 million to their campaigns, which constituted 12 percent of the total monies raised to that point in the campaign, and most states had not yet begun to hold their primary contests.[25] Furthermore, this total did not include much of the money that Jon Corzine, a former Wall Street investment banker and candidate for the Democratic nomination in the New Jersey Senate race, had spent on his bid for office. By the time Corzine won the June primary, he had already spent close to $35 million of his own money on the campaign, or about $7 million more than the record amount of personal money Huffington spent in the 1994 Senate race in California.[26] If this rate of self-financing continues, the total for 2000 is likely to surpass that of any previous election.

As these data for 2000 suggest, the extent to which candidates have come to rely on their own personal wealth is even more pronounced when all candidates are considered rather than general election candidates alone. The entire pool of congressional candidates in 1998 contributed or loaned $107.2 million of their own funds, which was slightly more than the $106.6 million in personal funding reported in 1996.[27] Approximately 18.6 percent of the monies raised by Senate candidates, $53.5 million, came from the candidates' own pockets, as did about 10.7 percent of the money in House races, or a total of $52.2 million. Moreover, even these figures understate the role of personal wealth in these contests. During the course of a campaign, some candidates pay off loans that they make to jump-start their candidacies, and the final figures on candidate contributions simply reflect any outstanding loans that have not been repaid by the end of the election cycle. In 1996, for example, six Senate candidates and nineteen House candidates had each repaid at least $100,000 in money loaned to their campaigns before the final spending reports were filed.

Almost all of the money contributed by candidates comes from challengers or individuals contesting open seats. Since 1988, less than 2 percent of the funds raised by incumbents seeking reelection to the House or Senate came from their own monies. In 1998, only one Senate and two House incumbents gave $100,000 or more to their campaigns. In contrast, personal funds accounted for 37 percent of the monies raised by Senate challengers and 24 percent of the monies raised by House challengers. In open-seat contests, 23 percent of the funding in Senate races and 26 percent of the funding for House races came from the candidates' own resources.

In recent elections, self-financed candidates also have become a feature of the presidential race. Indeed, the best-known example of a wealthy challenger is H. Ross Perot, who spent close to $64 million of his personal wealth to finance his bid for the presidency in 1992. In 1996, he spent an additional $8.2 million in support of the Reform Party, under whose banner he once again ran for president. In 1996, two candidates also spent large sums of their own money seeking the White House. Malcolm "Steve" Forbes catapulted into the top tier of contenders on the strength of the $37 million he spent on his campaign, most of which he contributed himself. Another contender, Maurice Taylor, president of Titan Wheel International, spent $6.5 million but was less successful in launching his candidacy.[28]

Self-financing has become increasingly popular because it offers candidates a number of advantages. If a candidate can afford to contribute or loan $100,000 or $250,000 or even more to his or her campaign, he or she will have the "seed money" needed to launch a campaign and perhaps gain the credibility needed to be recognized as a serious candidate by political insiders and even members of the public at large. In addition, a candidate who can rely on personal funds does not have to incur the substantial costs that accompany the start of a fundraising effort and thus will have more money available to spend on other campaign activities than an opponent who is not self-financing. Finally, a candidate who relies exclusively or largely on personal funds for campaign money is not constrained by FECA contribution limits. Personal contributions or loans are not limited by the FECA, since the court in *Buckley* ruled that there is no concern about corruption in this form of financing. As a result, the only limit on a candidate's personal contribution is the limit on how much of his or her own money the candidate is willing to spend.

The growing importance of personal wealth raises serious questions about the role of money in our political system. One recent study of 1992–98 House primary campaigns by Jennifer Steen, which encompassed more than 1,600 nonincumbent candidates who raised at least $50,000 and ran in districts where their party's normal vote share was at least 40 percent, found that the self-investments of inexperienced candidates reduced the number of experienced candidates who decided to contest a seat by about 15 percent. In open-seat races, the effect was slightly greater, reducing the number of experienced candidates by about 16 percent from the number that would have been expected in the absence of any candidate self-financing.[29] Indeed, the potential financial advantage offered by a wealthy challenger has encouraged party leaders to seek out such candidates to run against better-known, better-financed incumbents. The long-term effect of this development may therefore be to increase the number of wealthy individuals who seek office.

But this financial advantage enjoyed by wealthy challengers does not always translate into victory at polls. In 1996, only 19 of the 145 Senate and House candidates who contributed $100,000 or more to their campaigns were successful on election day. And the biggest spenders, Democrat Mark Warner of Virginia, who gave $10.3 million to his Senate campaign, and Republican Guy Millner of Georgia, who gave $6.4 million to his Senate campaign, both lost. Similarly, in 1998, only 11 of the 87 Senate and House candidates who gave $100,000 or more to their campaigns were successful. So, while self-financed challengers do have better odds of winning a race, the advantage is not overwhelming. For example, Steen determined that $100,000 in self-financing improved a challenger's prospect of winning by only 2.7 percent, but $1 million in self-financing improved the chance of winning by 16.3 percent. The benefit of self-investment was greatest in open-seat contests, where $1 million in personal funding increased the predicted chance of winning by 38 percent.[30] These results demonstrate that personal wealth does have an effect, although not as significant an effect as some might claim.

HOW DO THESE PATTERNS OF FUNDING AFFECT ELECTORAL COMPETITION?

In 1974, the average amount spent by a House incumbent in the primary and general election campaigns was $111,000, while the average for their general election opponents was about $75,000. By 1998, this gap had grown considerably, with incumbents spending an average of almost $633,000, as opposed to about $252,000 for challengers who made it to the general election. In Senate contests, incumbents in 1974 spent an average of about $1.3 million, almost twice the $698,000 spent by their general election opponents. By 1998, Senate incumbents were spending an average of about $4.7 million as opposed to $2.7 million for their opponents. The average spending margin in House races between officeholders and their opponents has thus grown from about $36,000 in 1974 to almost $380,000 in 1998. In Senate races, the average margin during the same period has grown from about $600,000 to $2 million.[31]

The scope of the disparity in resources available to incumbents and challengers has led many observers to conclude that money is a major factor in explaining the high reelection rates among incumbents. A study of the 1992 election by Common Cause, for example, found that 290 of the 349 congressional incumbents who ran in the general election were either unopposed or faced a challenger who had less than one-half as much money to spend. In the forty-eight races in which an incumbent won with less than 55 percent of the vote, the challengers were outspent by a margin of more than three to one ($10 million for the challengers as compared to $34 million for the incumbents). This analysis suggested that superior finances were the reason why most incumbents were reelected.[32]

An analysis of the 1998 elections conducted by the Center for Responsive Politics also concluded that the ability to outspend an opponent is the key to election victory.[33] This review found that more than nine out of ten House and Senate candidates who spent more than their opponents were victorious at the polls. Moreover, it revealed that many of the races, particularly for the House, were financially uncompetitive. In more than 60 percent of House districts, one candidate outspent the other by a margin of ten to one or more. None of the candidates who spent less in these races won. In all, only twenty-five races were won by candidates who did not outspend their opponents, and in twenty-two of these contests, the disparity in spending was a margin of two to one or less.

These findings and other, similar analyses have led many advocates of campaign finance reform to conclude that money plays a major role in determining electoral outcomes and that limits on spending are the key to improving the competitiveness of elections. Money, however, is not everything. There are many factors that influence election results, including the quality of the candidates, the state of the economy, and the national political environment.

In addition, it is not the case that challengers have to outspend their opponents in order to win election. Although the amount of money spent by incumbents has an influence on voting results,[34] many academic studies have concluded that the amount spent by challengers is a more important factor in determining the competitiveness of elections. Money means more to a challenger than an incumbent because a challenger is usually less well known and must be able to communicate effectively with the electorate in order to mount a competitive campaign. A challenger must therefore raise the sum needed to meet this objective; he or she does not necessarily have to match the spending of an incumbent in order to win election.

This conclusion is supported by the experience in recent elections. In 1992, for example, challengers who defeated incumbents spent an average of $451,000, while the incumbents they defeated spent on average more than twice as much, about $965,000. Furthermore, challengers fare better at the polls in relationship to their ability to raise funds: those who received 40 to 49 percent of the vote spent an average of $281,000 versus about $90,000 for those who received less than 40 percent of the vote. Conversely, incumbents who won with more than 60 percent of the vote spent an average of $487,000, or half as much as those who lost.[35] Similarly, a study of the 1998 congressional elections found that seven of the nine challengers who beat House or Senate incumbents spent less than their opponents. Those challengers who received 40 percent or more of the vote typically spent in excess of $300,000, while those who received less than 40 percent of the vote typically spent less than $200,000.[36] But these relatively low thresholds were achieved by few candidates. In 1998, only 106 challengers, about a third of those competing against House members, managed to raise $200,000.[37]

The financial patterns evident in 1992 and 1998 were not unique. A survey of the 1,540 House races from 1976 to 1990 in which an incumbent faced a major party challenger in successive elections concluded that, while money is essential, challengers do not as a rule have to spend as much as incumbents to win.[38] What challengers have to do is raise enough money to be able to wage a meaningful campaign. The problem under current practices is that few of these candidates do so. Accordingly, many observers have concluded that the predominant problem in the campaign finance system is not so much the large sums raised by incumbents but rather the inadequate resources available to challengers.[39] These observers therefore tend to promote proposals that would provide challengers with greater resources, such as public funding, higher contribution limits, and free television time.

5

THE PRESIDENTIAL PUBLIC
FINANCING SYSTEM

The most innovative component of the 1974 FECA was the system of voluntary public financing for presidential candidates. This program provides
taxpayer-financed subsidies to presidential candidates in the prenomination
and general election campaigns, as well as subsidies to national party committees for presidential nomination conventions. The program matches the
small contributions raised by qualified candidates in the prenomination campaign and provides full funding for major party nominees and partial funding
for other qualified candidates in the general election. To qualify for these subsidies, candidates must demonstrate a threshold level of public support and
agree to abide by spending limits. Party committees receive a convention subsidy based on a sum established by federal law.

Funding for the public financing program comes from a tax checkoff on
the federal income tax form. Through 1992, this checkoff provision allowed
tax filers to designate one dollar (or two dollars for joint filers) for deposit in
the Presidential Election Campaign Fund (PECF), a separate account maintained by the U.S. Treasury Department, which is used to make payouts for
public financing. In 1993, the amount of the checkoff was increased to three

dollars (or six dollars for joint filers) in order to account for the effects of inflation since 1976 and better meet the growing financial demands of the public funding system. Public participation through the checkoff is encouraged by placing no direct cost on the taxpayer: the decision to contribute to the PECF has no effect on an individual's tax liability or on the size of any refund—it simply lets the government know that the amount checked off should be deposited in the separate Treasury account.

WHAT ARE THE RULES GOVERNING PUBLICLY FINANCED PRESIDENTIAL CAMPAIGNS?

Presidential candidates who accept public money are subject to different rules than those governing congressional challengers. In addition to the FECA's disclosure rules and contribution limits, publicly funded presidential hopefuls must agree to abide by spending limits and to restrict personal contributions to their own campaigns to $50,000.

In primary elections, presidential candidates are eligible for public matching funds if they fulfill certain fundraising requirements. These requirements have not changed since the law was adopted. To qualify, a candidate must raise at least $5,000 in contributions of $250 or less in at least twenty states. Once this threshold is achieved, public subsidies are granted on a dollar-for-dollar basis on the first $250 contributed by each individual. The maximum amount a candidate for the nomination may receive in public money is a sum equal to one-half of the overall primary spending limit. The spending limit was set in 1974 at $10 million with adjustments for inflation, plus an additional 20 percent for fundraising costs. By 1996, this overall primary spending ceiling had grown to $30.9 million, plus $6.2 million for fundraising costs. Candidates also may raise and spend an unlimited amount for "compliance costs," which are legal and accounting expenses incurred to comply with the law. In addition to this overall spending limit, the law sets ceilings on the amount a candidate may spend in each state, based on the state's voting-age population with adjustments for inflation. In 1996, these limits ranged from $618,200 in small states such as New Hampshire and Delaware to $11.3 million in California.[1]

In the general election, major party nominees can receive a full public subsidy equal to the total amount of the general election expenditure ceiling. The amount of this subsidy was set at $20 million in 1974 with adjustments for inflation; by 1996, it had increased to $61.8 million. As a condition of receiving this subsidy, candidates must agree that they will not raise and spend additional private monies for their campaign committees (except to finance legal and accounting costs). Minor party candidates can qualify for a proportional share of this subsidy based on the share of the vote they received in the previous election as compared to the average vote received by the major parties. New parties and minor parties also can qualify for postelection subsidies on the same proportional basis, so long as they receive at least 5 percent of the vote. Thus, in 1996 Ross Perot qualified for $29.2 million in public funding for his general election campaign, based on his performance in the 1992 election, in which he gained 19 percent of the vote.[2]

Finally, national party committees have the option of receiving public funds to subsidize the cost of their presidential nominating conventions. Each major party can receive a basic grant that was originally set in 1974 at $2 million plus adjustments for inflation and was subsequently increased to $3 million in 1979 and $4 million in 1984. With adjustments for inflation, the total amount of the subsidy for each party reached $12.4 million by 1996. Minor parties that hold national nominating conventions also can qualify for convention funding in lesser amounts, based on their proportionate share of the vote in the previous election.

HAS THE TAX CHECKOFF BEEN A SUCCESSFUL FUNDING MECHANISM?

In the six presidential elections from 1976 to 1996, the tax checkoff provided $891 million in financing for presidential campaigns. A total of $256.6 million was distributed to 74 primary candidates, $92.7 million to the 2 major parties for 12 nominating conventions, and $541.6 million in general election funding for 12 major party nominees and 2 nonmajor party candidates (John Anderson in 1980 and Ross Perot in 1996). Of the $891 million total, $432.7 million went to Republicans (for 25 primary candidates, 6 general election tickets, and 6 conventions), $421 million went to Democrats (for 44 primary candidates, 6 general election tickets, and 6 conventions), and $37.2 million went to minor party candidates (5 in primaries and 2 in general elections).[3]

The amount of money expended through the public financing program has increased with each election cycle (see Table 5.1, page 56). In 1976, the PECF disbursed about $72 million in subsidies; in 1980, $99 million; in 1988, $178 million; and in 1996, $232 million, or more than three times the sum disbursed twenty years earlier. This growth is largely due to the structure of the public financing system: because the spending ceilings are indexed for inflation, the amount of money candidates may receive from the fund increases with each new cycle. In addition, in recent elections the number of primary contenders capable of raising large sums of money has increased, thereby

TABLE 5.1
PRESIDENTIAL ELECTION
CAMPAIGN FUND PAYMENTS ($ MILLIONS)

	1976	1980	1984	1988	1992	1996
Convention	4.4	8.8	16.2	18.4	22.1	24.7
General Election	43.6	58.9	80.8	92.2	110.5	152.7
Primary	24.3	31.5	36.5	67.5	41.8	58.5
TOTAL	72.3	99.2	133.5	178.1	174.4	235.9

Source: Based on data reported by the Federal Election Commission.

increasing the demand for public matching funds. Another factor in the recent growth is the participation of minor party candidates, who have qualified for matching funds and, in the case of the Reform party, general election subsidies.

While demand for public money has been increasing, the amount contributed by taxpayers has been on the decline. Although the early years of the checkoff were characterized by rising participation and substantial growth in the annual revenues deposited in the PECF, this trend peaked in 1981, when 28.7 percent of all tax returns designated a contribution to the program for a total deposit of $41 million. Since then, reported rates of participation and revenues have declined, falling to 18.9 percent and less than $28 million in 1993 and thereafter even lower (see Table 5.2).

In 1993, Congress sought to address the financial pressures facing the PECF by tripling the amount of a checkoff contribution to three dollars (or six dollars on a joint return). This amendment was designed to adjust the checkoff to account for the effects of inflation since 1974. But since this change was made, the percentage of returns that designate a contribution to the PECF has declined further. In 1994, only 14.5 percent of tax returns included a contribution to the Fund, which led to a total deposit of $71.3 million, or about $11 million less than a tripling of the 1993 deposit would have produced. By 1997, the participation rate had dropped to 12.4 percent and the total contribution to about $66.4 million.

The combination of rising costs and declining annual revenues led to concerns in advance of both the 1992 and 1996 elections that the public financing program would lack the money needed to meet all of the demands for funding. These concerns were exacerbated by the operating mechanics of the program. By law, the Treasury Department must set aside the monies needed for anticipated general election and convention financing before distributing any monies to primary candidates in the form of matching funds. Most

TABLE 5.2
FEDERAL INCOME TAX CHECKOFF

Calendar Year	Percentage of Returns with Checkoff[a]	Dollar Amount Designated ($ Millions)	Fund Balance ($ Millions)[b]
1999[c]	—	61.1	165.5
1998	12.5	63.3	133.2
1997	12.6	66.3	69.9
1996	12.9	66.9	3.7
1995	13.0	67.9	146.9
1994[d]	14.5	71.3	101.7
1993	18.9	27.6	30.8
1992	17.7	29.6	4.1
1991	19.5	32.3	127.1
1990	19.8	32.5	115.4
1989	20.1	32.3	82.9
1988	21.0	33.0	52.5
1987	21.7	33.7	177.9
1986	23.0	35.8	161.7
1985	23.0	34.7	125.9
1984	23.7	35.0	92.7
1983	24.2	35.6	177.3
1982	27.0	39.0	153.4
1981	28.7	41.0	114.4
1980	27.4	38.8	73.7
1979	25.4	35.9	135.2
1978	28.6	39.2	100.3
1977	27.5	36.6	60.9
1976	25.5	33.7	23.8
1975	24.2	31.7	59.6
1974[e]	—	27.6	27.6
1973[e]	—	2.4	2.4

Cont. on next page

a The percentages refer to the tax returns of the previous year. For example, the 12.5 percent of
the 1997 tax returns that included a checkoff contribution directed $63.3 million into the
Presidential Election Campaign Fund in calendar year 1998.
b Figures represent the amount of money in the Presidential Election Campaign Fund at the end
of the year.
c Percentage of returns not yet available.
d In 1993, Congress increased the amount of the checkoff from $1 to $3 (or from $2 to $6 on a
joint return). The 1994 contributions were the first under the higher checkoff amount.
e The 1973 tax forms were the first to have the checkoff on the first page; in 1972, taxpayers had
to file a separate form to exercise the checkoff option. To compensate for the presumed difficulty
caused by the separate form, taxpayers were allowed to designate $1 for 1972 as well as 1973 on
the 1973 forms. Given these circumstances, total and percentage figures would be misleading.

Source: Based on data reported by the Federal Election Commission.

of the annual revenues, however, are received during the height of the tax
filing season, late March and early April, or more than a month after the presidential primaries have begun. This set-aside provision thus intensifies the
financial pressures placed on the PECF at the start of the presidential selection
process because it does not allow administrators to pay for the primary campaigns first and then rely on the tax checkoff monies received during the election year to finance the general election. Instead, the only monies available to
primary candidates are those left over after the general election money and
convention payments are secured.

In 1996, despite the increase in the size of the checkoff, the PECF did
experience a shortfall during the primary campaign, and candidates received
only a percentage of the public subsidies they had earned during the crucial
early months of the presidential contest. The first 1996 matching fund payments, which were distributed on January 1, 1996, represented only 60 percent
of the funding to which the candidates were entitled.[4] In most cases, candidates compensated for the lack of public revenues by securing bank loans
against the matching funds owed them, which were repaid when the Fund
overcame the shortfall in April.

Early estimates for the 2000 election indicated that the PECF would
experience a more significant shortfall than it did in 1996. In mid-1999, the
FEC predicted that on January 1, 2000, the Fund was expected to be able to
pay only about thirty-two cents on the dollar for the matching funds earned by
the candidates.[5] By year-end, however, the situation was seen as not so dire, in
large part because two of the leading Republican candidates chose to forgo
public funding. Governor George Bush of Texas raised over $56 million by
the end of September 1999 and decided to rely on his campaign's extraordinary
fundraising success to spend as much as he could raise. He thus decided not to
take public money so that he would not be subject to spending limits.

Republican Steve Forbes also decided to eschew public funds, choosing once again to rely primarily on his personal resources to finance his campaign. By the end of September, he had raised more than $20 million, including $16.3 million of his own money. As a result, the amounts requested by candidates were lower than anticipated, with eight presidential candidates certified to receive $34.0 million in initial matching fund payments in January 2000, as compared to $37.4 million for ten candidates in 1996.[6]

The PECF will have even less money available in 2004 than in 2000 if current checkoff trends continue. As a result, there may be relatively little money available for matching fund payments to candidates at the start of the presidential selection process in 2004. Candidates will therefore have less incentive to participate in the program and accept the spending limits that public subsidies entail. In short, the matching funds program may begin to collapse.

The decline in tax checkoff participation rates is at the center of the financial problems facing the public funding program and is often cited by critics as evidence of the public's lack of support for public funding. But the decline in participation may not be as steep or as steady as is often assumed. According to one analysis, between 1983 and 1991, when the rate of participation fell from 24.2 percent to 19.5 percent, the actual number of tax returns that earmarked a contribution remained relatively stable, ranging from 23.2 million to 22.3 million. In three of those years—1986, 1988, and 1990—the number of participants was higher than in the previous year. This suggests that the sharpness of the decline is not due simply to the number of participants; it is also a function of the increase in the number of returns filed each year.[7] Similarly, in recent years, participation under the three-dollar checkoff has been relatively stable, ranging from 13.0 percent in 1994 to 12.4 percent in 1997.[8]

Although a majority of the public does not contribute through the checkoff, it is important to note that this means of contributing has significantly expanded the number of individuals who participate financially in the political process. About 80 percent of those who use the checkoff do not contribute to candidates, party committees, or political organizations. Indeed, the share of the public (as opposed to the number of tax returns) that reports making a contribution through the federal checkoff is greater than 20 percent, or almost four times the percentage who report making a donation to a candidate or political committee.[9] So even though checkoff participation is generally considered to be low, this means of contributing is the most popular form of financial participation in the electoral process.

While opponents of public funding usually assume that declining participation is a reflection of public attitudes toward public financing, this behavior reflects a number of different factors. First, there is a notable lack of awareness among taxpayers of the checkoff and how the program works. Second, there has been a significant increase in the number of taxpayers who use an accountant or tax preparer, and half of tax filers now use such services.[10] These tax returns show a substantially higher rate of nonparticipation, which has led some to conclude that preparers do not highlight the checkoff.[11] Finally, an estimated 13 million taxpayers, about one-fifth of those who do their own returns, now use computer software.[12] At least some of these programs default to empty checkoff boxes, which may produce nonparticipation by oversight or neglect.

Whatever the reason for the current levels of participation, it is clear that reform of the checkoff program is needed if the future financial health of the program is to be ensured. The FEC has suggested that the Treasury Department reinterpret the rules when beginning its payments to take into account the deposits to be made during the election year. The Commission further suggests that Congress should change the payout priorities so that convention funding is last rather than first among the categories, which would guarantee that matching funds are available before money is set aside for the conventions.[13] Another option is to eliminate the convention subsidy altogether since parties still raise large sums from private contributions and spend far more than the amount of the subsidy on their conventions. Congress also could eliminate the checkoff altogether and simply finance the program through the annual appropriations process, as is the case in some state public funding schemes. This approach, however, might place the funding at even greater risk than under the checkoff since it might become a focal point for partisan battles over budget priorities.

HOW HAS PUBLIC FUNDING AFFECTED THE FINANCING OF PRESIDENTIAL CAMPAIGNS?

While a majority of taxpayers have not participated in the public funding program, a majority of candidates have. In fact, public financing has gained widespread acceptance among those seeking the nation's highest office.

Every major party presidential ticket since 1976 has relied on public money to finance its general election campaign. Of those who have sought the major party nominations, only five Republicans (John Connally in 1980, Maurice Taylor in 1996, Steve Forbes in 1996 and 2000, and George W. Bush and Orrin Hatch in 2000) have chosen not to participate. In addition, independent candidate Ross Perot chose not to participate in the public funding in his bid for the presidency in 1992. Of these nonparticipants, three (Perot, Forbes, and Taylor) opted out in large part because this would allow them to use unlimited amounts of their personal wealth. Perot spent $63.3 million of his own money seeking the presidency in 1992. Forbes put up more than $30 million in his failed quest for the 1996 Republican nomination, and Maurice Taylor, one of Forbes's opponents, tried to jump-start a campaign by contributing $6.5 million from his own pocket.[14]

Presidential aspirants have embraced public subsidies because these have proved to be an invaluable resource. The general election grants alone have drastically reduced the amount of time candidates have to spend raising money. Without public financing, candidates would have to spend most of their time between July and November raising funds in order to accrue the tens of millions of dollars needed to mount a national campaign. Public funding also has helped to hold down campaign costs since candidates do not have to spend the millions of dollars on fundraising that would be needed to generate the more than $60 million provided by public funding.

Primary election matching funds have been an important source of revenue for presidential candidates as well. In each election since 1976, approximately a third of all the monies raised by those seeking presidential nomination has come from public subsidies. Candidates who emphasize small individual contributions usually receive 40 percent or more of their funding from public monies. Even those who emphasize the solicitation of larger gifts of $500 or more, such as incumbent vice presidents or well-established candidates, usually receive 25 to 30 percent of their total revenues from public monies.

Public financing has particularly benefited the more ideological and lesser-known individuals who have sought the presidency. Liberal candidates such as Democrats Jesse Jackson in 1984 and 1988 and Jerry Brown in 1992 have received the vast majority of their campaign funds from smaller donations and thus qualified for substantial amounts of public money. For example, Jackson raised a combined $17.4 million from individuals in his two bids for the presidency and earned $10.7 million in matching funds; Brown accepted only small individual donations and raised $5.2 million that qualified for $4.2 million in matching monies. Similarly, conservative candidates such as Republicans Pat Robertson in 1988 and Patrick Buchanan in 1992 have received large sums of public money in their bids for the presidency by successfully soliciting contributions from a broad base of small donors. Robertson raised $20.6 million in 1988 and earned $9.7 million in matching funds. Buchanan raised $7.2 million in 1992, which generated $5.0 million in matching funds. Another, more established conservative who received substantial help from public funding was President Ronald Reagan, who received about 60 percent of the funds for his 1984 reelection campaign from small donors and, as a result, earned $9.7 million in matching funds, which was the maximum amount of public matching money allowed a candidate under the law at that time.[15]

Public funding of primary campaigns also has helped lesser-known challengers by providing them with the revenues needed to mount a competitive contest or raise the additional funding needed to wage a serious campaign in the critical, early primary states. For these individuals, such as Jimmy Carter in 1976, Gary Hart in 1984, Bill Clinton and Paul Tsongas in 1992, and John McCain in 2000, public subsidies provided sorely needed revenues at crucial points in the delegate selection contest to help them continue in the race or communicate their ideas to voters.[16] Public funding has thus played some role in enhancing competition in presidential primary campaigns.

That lesser-known candidates and those from outside the mainstream of the major parties have benefited from public funding is not to claim that more well-known candidates have been unduly disadvantaged by the program. Well-known candidates, especially those perceived as front-runners, also benefit from matching subsidies. Because these candidates usually enter the race with an established base of broad financial support, they can solicit a greater number of small donations or matchable contributions than can their opponents. By doing so, they can significantly increase the financial advantage they hold over lesser-known challengers. In most instances, public funding provides a larger amount of money to better-known contenders and thus helps them maintain their financial superiority in a presidential race.

HAS PUBLIC FINANCING ENCOURAGED CANDIDATES TO SOLICIT SMALL CONTRIBUTIONS?

One of the basic objectives of the FECA's public funding program was to encourage presidential candidates to expand their bases of financial support and, by providing matching funds for the first $250 given by an individual, to place greater reliance on small individual donations. The law has certainly had this effect; serious contenders for the presidential nomination now must solicit contributions from tens of thousands of donors in order to raise the money needed to mount a viable campaign.

However, in recent elections a growing number of candidates have placed greater emphasis on the solicitation of larger gifts—$500 or more—in building their campaign war chests. In 1980, only Jimmy Carter, an incumbent president seeking reelection, and Republican John Connally, who refused public funding, raised a greater share of their campaign monies from larger donations than from contributions of less than $500. In 1988 and 1992, almost half of the candidates for the major party nominations raised most of their money from large donors.

Yet, even with this increase in large givers, small donors are still an essential source of revenue in presidential campaigns. On average, larger donors are responsible for less than 50 percent of the individual money received in a presidential campaign, as compared to more than 50 percent in House races and more than 60 percent in Senate races.

HAS PUBLIC FINANCING REDUCED THE FUNDRAISING PRESSURES ON FEDERAL CANDIDATES?

The public funding program was designed to relieve candidates of some of the pressures placed on them to raise money, and the program has certainly had this effect in general election campaigns. The program has also helped to reduce the amounts of money candidates have to raise on their own in seeking a presidential nomination. But fundraising pressures have increased in recent elections due to a structural imbalance in the law and changes in the presidential selection process.

The FECA adjusts *spending* limits for inflation but not *contribution* limits. Thus, the amount a candidate is legally allowed to spend in a presidential nomination bid has grown from $12 million to more than $40 million, but the maximum amount an individual may legally contribute has remained flat at $1,000. So in each succeeding election, candidates have been allowed to raise larger amounts, spending more time and money in order to generate the increasingly large number of small contributions needed to raise the amount legally allowed by the rising spending limit. The beneficial effects of the law with respect to candidate fundraising have been mitigated by the inequity built into the law. Instead of reducing the amount of time candidates have to devote to raising money, the effect of the law has been to increase it.

The potential benefits of the FECA have been further diminished by the strategic realities generated by changes in the presidential selection process. Throughout the 1980s and 1990s, the presidential primary calendar has become "front-loaded," as a growing number of states have decided to hold their elections in the period from mid-February to the end of March. This phenomenon has increased the financial demands at the start of the formal presidential selection process substantially, which, in turn, has compelled candidates to raise more and more money before the first votes are cast. The campaign finance laws were not designed with such a system in mind, and the result has been a need for candidates to begin raising money earlier and earlier in the year before the elections take place.

This need to raise money early has become particularly acute in the 2000 election cycle since a number of the largest, most expensive states, including

California and New York, have moved their primaries to early March in an effort to exert more influence on the nomination. This contraction of the selection period has not only increased the costs of the earliest stage of the selection process (the period from mid-February to mid-March), but it also has made it necessary for candidates to run campaigns in more than a dozen states simultaneously, with practically no time to reload their campaign coffers between Iowa and New Hampshire and the next wave of primary contests. Candidates therefore have to raise almost all of the money needed for the first month of primaries well in advance of the start of the formal selection process. In 2000, most experts estimated that a candidate needed to raise about $21 million before the first votes were cast in order to have the funds needed to run a top-tier campaign.[17]

HAVE SPENDING LIMITS BEEN EFFECTIVE IN REDUCING THE COST OF CAMPAIGNS?

Under the terms of the FECA, any candidate who accepts public funding must abide by spending limits. Assessments of the presidential public financing system are therefore often linked with judgments on the benefits of spending limits, particularly since the Supreme Court's decision in *Buckley*, which ruled that expenditure limits are allowable only if they are part of a system of voluntary public subsidies. Accordingly, one of the appeals of public financing has been its role as an inducement for candidates to accept limits on spending.

The basic objective behind the spending limits is to reduce the cost of presidential campaigns, and there has been some moderation in presidential spending since the limits were put in place. Since 1976, presidential spending has not increased as rapidly as spending in House or Senate elections. And there have been a number of cases where particular candidates have had to reduce their levels of spending in order to accommodate the ceilings. At least seven candidates have had to cut back significantly on anticipated expenditures or were reluctant to spend available funds because of the aggregate limit: Republicans Gerald Ford and Ronald Reagan in 1976, Reagan again in 1980, Democrat Walter Mondale in 1984, Republican George Bush in 1988, Democrat Bill Clinton in 1992, and Republican Robert Dole in 1996.

However, a growing number of candidates in recent elections have either violated the law or sought ways to avoid its constraints. In almost every election since 1984, at least one of the leading candidates or nominees has exceeded the aggregate primary spending limit, while a number of challengers have exceeded the limit in at least one of the states (usually in Iowa or New Hampshire, the first two contests). In 1988, for example, eight candidates surpassed the spending limit in Iowa by an average of $360,000, while six candidates violated the limit in New Hampshire by an average of $219,000.[18]

The penalties for exceeding a spending limit are not severe—candidates simply have to pay a penalty, usually issued a year or more after an election, equal to the percentage of the excess spending that represents the expenditure of public money, which is usually about 33 percent. There is therefore little incentive to comply with the limits. What incentive does exist is a result of the fear many candidates have of news reports during the primaries. Most contenders do not want to face news stories that claim he or she has "broken the law," or that he or she is close to the spending limit and therefore in a strategically vulnerable position because an opponent may be able to spend more. They therefore try to avoid reaching the limit before the voting is over.

Even those candidates who do respect the spending limits and seek to abide by the law find this task to be increasingly onerous given the realities of presidential campaigning. The fundraising pressures felt by candidates encourage an early start to campaigning, but this practice conflicts with the objectives of the spending limit, which encourage candidates to restrict their early expenses and limit the scope of their campaigning. In each succeeding election, candidates therefore find it more and more difficult to raise the money they need early yet remain within the spending limits. Those who do manage both tasks successfully, especially those who win a contested nomination, often find themselves in the position of having little left to spend in the months before the convention. Robert Dole, for example, had the Republican nomination wrapped up by early April of 1996, but in doing so he had spent most of the amount allowed under the spending limit. By contrast, his opponent, President Bill Clinton, was uncontested for the Democratic nomination. Clinton therefore had about $20 million left to spend in the months before the convention, while Dole was essentially broke.[19]

These concerns—the prospect of violating the law, incurring political "penalties," or being placed at a financial disadvantage—have increasingly compelled candidates to find ways to avoid the limits. This has led to a wide array of ingenious and inventive tactics that have allowed candidates to circumvent the law altogether or engage in creative accounting that has allowed them to avoid any penalty under the FECA. Consequently, the principal effect of the limits has not been to control the cost of campaigns; instead, they have given candidates, especially presidential nominees, an incentive to find new ways of spending money outside the law.

One of the most common ways primary challengers have found to evade the law is to establish a precandidacy PAC or advocacy organization that can essentially serve as a shadow campaign organization. Because a PAC or advocacy group is a legally separate entity from a presidential campaign committee, it is not subject to the contribution and spending limits imposed on qualified presidential candidates. Even if a potential candidate heads a PAC, the money raised and spent by the committee is not considered to be a presidential campaign expense, so long as that individual or PAC avoids a few specific activities that the FEC regards as signs of an official candidacy.[20]

The use of these precandidacy organizations has made a mockery of the primary spending limits. In 1980, four Republican candidates, beginning with Ronald Reagan, employed this device; in 1984, Reagan used it once again, as did four Democratic hopefuls, including the eventual party nominee, Walter Mondale; in 1988, ten of the thirteen major party candidates established committees before becoming candidates. During this period, the total amounts raised and spent by these shadow organizations rose from about $7.5 million in advance of the 1980 election to $25.2 million in the years before the 1988 election.[21]

This practice has continued throughout the 1990s. In anticipation of the 2000 election, at least seven presidential hopefuls had already established PACs or advocacy organizations as of November 1997. By this time these committees had raised more than $7 million and spent the money on such activities as polling in New Hampshire and Iowa, fundraising, political travel, and contributions to state and local candidates.[22] The candidates counted none of these monies against federal campaign limits.

Another effective means of circumventing the limits, particularly during the general election campaign, is to rely on party committees, since these committees can now engage in the types of financial activity that the FECA and public financing program were supposed to abolish. Party organizations have learned that they can pay for many of the activities that will clearly benefit the campaign of a presidential nominee or other federal candidate, including such campaign staples as voter identification and turnout programs, campaign paraphernalia, and some types of advertising, without having to count these expenses against the presidential spending ceilings or coordinated expenditure limits.

Consequently, the level playing field that was supposed to have been created by the adoption of spending ceilings has never been realized in practice. While some candidates have spent less than they could have because of the limits, and some have been fined for violating the limits, the law has had little effect in controlling the costs of presidential campaigns. This experience has heightened the controversy surrounding spending limits as a vehicle of campaign finance reform since it has led many to the conclusion that limits are not an effective means of regulation, while others have defended the idea of limits and argued that they can work if the primary means of circumventing the law are thwarted, especially the new financial practices of the party organizations.

6

PARTY FINANCING AND SOFT MONEY

Traditionally, parties played a major role in the financing of elections. But this party-centered finance system gradually declined in the 1950s and 1960s, as campaigns became more candidate-centered and media-oriented, and candidates and their personal campaign organizations assumed most of the responsibility for raising funds.

Over the past two decades, the national party committees have once again assumed an active role in the financing of federal election campaigns. This renewed activity is in part due to their improved fundraising success under the rules established by the FECA and in part a result of a highly controversial, new form of party finance, "soft money," which was not anticipated by the reforms of the 1970s and is now generally regarded as the greatest problem in the campaign finance system.

WHAT IS THE DIFFERENCE BETWEEN PARTY "HARD MONEY" AND "SOFT MONEY"?

The Republican and Democratic national party committees raise two types of money, which are commonly referred to as "hard money" and "soft money." Hard money is the money raised under federal contribution limits for use in federal elections. This federal funding comes from the voluntary contributions made by individuals, PACs, and state and local party committees to the party organizations that are regulated by the FECA, including the Democratic National Committee (DNC), Republican National Committee (RNC), Democratic Senatorial Campaign Committee (DSCC), National Republican Senatorial Committee (NRSC), Democratic Congressional Campaign Committee (DCCC), and National Republican Congressional Committee (NRCC). Hard money can be used for any purpose and is the only funding that can be used to finance activities that directly benefit and advocate the election or defeat of federal candidates, such as candidate contributions, coordinated expenditures, and independent expenditures.

Soft money, as noted earlier, is the money raised by national party committees to finance party-building activities and other expenditures, such as administrative costs or contributions to state and local candidates. Because these funds are generally not used for activities that expressly advocate the election or defeat of particular federal candidates, they are not considered federal election–related spending under the law and therefore are not subject to the contribution and expenditure limits established by the FECA. National party committees can therefore raise and spend unlimited amounts of soft money. They also may solicit unlimited soft money contributions from sources that are banned from making contributions to candidates under federal law, such as labor unions and corporations.

HOW MUCH DO THE PARTIES SPEND?

The monies raised by the national party committees have grown substantially since the FECA was adopted. In 1976, the Democratic and Republican party committees spent a total of about $59 million in hard money; by 1996, this sum had grown to almost $623 million, or more than ten times the amount spent twenty years earlier. Party committees spend less in midterm elections, but even in these election cycles the rise in expenditures has been impressive. In 1998, parties spent about $431 million, as compared to $113 million in 1978. Soft money expenditures grew at an even more rapid rate, rising from an estimated total of $19 million in 1980 to $271 million in 1996, an increase of more than fourteenfold in a sixteen-year period. In the 1998 midterm election, party committees spent almost $221 million in soft money, more than double the $103 million disbursed in 1994, which was the first midterm election in which the national party committees disclosed their soft money spending.

This pattern of increased party spending, especially the growth of soft money spending, will continue in 2000 and beyond. Because parties can now spend combinations of hard and soft money on a wide array of activities that benefit candidates, including such costly items as voter turnout programs, broadcast advertising, and direct mail efforts, they placed great emphasis on fundraising from the start of the 2000 election cycle, particularly with respect to soft money fundraising. Accordingly, by March 2000, the major party committees had already raised about $447 million, or about $78 million more than in the comparable period in 1996. All of this growth came in the form of soft money. The amount of hard money raised by the Democrats and Republicans in the first fifteen months of the 2000 cycle was about $1 million less than the amount raised during the first fifteen months of the 1996 cycle, with the Democrats raising $104 million, or about $800,000 more, and the Republicans raising $180 million, or about $2.1 million less than in 1996. The amount of soft money, however, almost doubled, from $85 million four years earlier to $163 million, with the Republicans receiving about $86 million and the Democrats, $77 million. Moreover, both parties were experiencing relatively equal increases in soft money receipts, with the Republicans' take up by 93 percent and the Democrats' up by 94 percent.[1] And these totals (see Table 6.1, page 70) did not include all the monies generated by the gala fundraising events held by each party later in the spring, which each raised more than $20 million for a one-night event. Given these revenues, party spending is certain to be significantly higher in 2000 than it was in 1996.

Overall, when hard and soft monies are combined, party spending has grown from $59 million in 1976 to more than $650 million in 1998. In other words, party spending has grown at a faster rate than the rate of increase in congressional election spending or in the total expenditures of all federal candidates. In 1996, the national party committees spent more ($894 million) than all congressional candidates combined ($765 million) and only about 20 percent less than the total amount spent by all congressional and presidential candidates ($1.1 billion).

There are substantial differences, however, in the amounts raised and spent by the two major parties. In general, the Republicans had a sizable financial advantage over the Democrats prior to the reforms of the 1970s, and their financial superiority has continued throughout the reform era. In 1976, the Republicans spent $40 million, as compared to $19 million for the Democrats, a margin of two to one. Over the next two decades, this revenue gap increased substantially. In 1996, the Republicans spent a total of $558 million, while the Democrats spent $336 million. In the 1998 midterm election, the Republicans spent close to $404 million, as compared to $248 million for the Democrats.

Most of the Republican financial advantage is due to the strength of their hard money fundraising. As noted in Table 6.1, in 1992, Republican party committees generated about $85 million more than the Democrats in hard

Table 6.1
National Political Party Spending, 1976–98 ($ Millions)

Election	Democrats			Republicans			Overall Spending		
	Federal (Hard)	Nonfederal (Soft)	Total	Federal (Hard)	Nonfederal (Soft)	Total	Federal (Hard)	Nonfederal (Soft)	Total
1976	19.4	—	19.4	40.1	—	40.1	59.5	—	59.5
1980	35.0	4.0	39.0	161.8	15.1	176.9	196.8	19.1	215.9
1984	97.4	6.0	103.4	300.8	15.6	316.4	398.2	21.6	419.8
1988	121.9	23.0	144.9	257.0	22.0	279.0	378.9	45.0	423.9
1992	171.9	32.9	204.8	256.1	47.5	303.6	428.0	80.4	508.4
1994	137.8	50.4	188.2	234.7	48.4	283.1	372.5	98.8	471.3
1996	214.3	121.8	336.1	408.5	149.7	558.2	622.8	271.5	894.3
1998	155.3	93.0	248.3	275.9	127.7	403.6	431.2	220.7	651.9

Sources: The 1976 figures are from Herbert E. Alexander, *Financing the 1976 Election* (Washington, D.C.: Congressional Quarterly, 1979), p. 190. Data on nonfederal funding from 1980 to 1988 are based on estimates reported in Anthony Corrado, *Paying for Presidents: Public Financing in National Elections* (New York: Twentieth Century Fund Press, 1993), p. 67. All other figures are based on data reported by the Federal Election Commission.

money but only $15 million more in soft money. In 1998, their relative advantage was $120 million in hard money and $35 million in soft money. So while the Republicans have done better than the Democrats in garnering soft money donations, their financial strength is largely a result of their success in generating federally regulated contributions.

These federal funds primarily come from small individual contributions. While individuals are allowed to give up to $20,000 per year to a national party committee, less than 1 percent of the more than one million individuals who donate money to national party committees each election cycle give anywhere near the legal maximum. Most of the money raised by the parties comes from individual gifts solicited through ongoing fundraising operations, primarily direct mail programs and telemarketing efforts. The average amount contributed by each of these donors is typically much less than $100.[2]

WHERE DOES SOFT MONEY COME FROM?

By contrast, the majority of soft money funds comes from large donations, especially gifts of $100,000 or more. In fact, the primary reason why soft money has grown so dramatically in recent elections—soft money expenditures rose from $45 million in 1988 to $80 million in 1992, and then tripled to $271 million in 1996—is that both parties have been very successful in soliciting large amounts from wealthy individuals, major corporations, and labor unions. Both the Democrats and Republicans have had organized programs to recruit donors of $100,000 or more since at least 1988, and in recent elections they have placed great emphasis on the solicitation of corporate contributions.

According to a recent analysis by the FEC, the parties are raising an increasingly large number of contributions from individuals in excess of federal limits or from sources that were supposed to be banned from participating in federal elections. During the 1992 election cycle, the national party committees' soft money accounts accepted at least 381 individual contributions in excess of $20,000 (the annual federal party contribution limit) and about 11,000 contributions from sources, particularly corporations and labor unions, that are prohibited from giving in federal elections. In the 1996 election cycle, both numbers more than doubled. During this election, the national party committees received nearly 1,000 contributions from individuals in excess of $20,000 and approximately 27,000 contributions from federally prohibited sources.[3]

The importance of corporate soft money contributions has been especially noteworthy. According to an analysis by the independent, nonpartisan Campaign Reform Project, individual donors account for less than a quarter of the soft money raised by the national party committees, providing a total of $20.4 million in 1994 and $42.9 million in 1998. Most of the soft money received by national party committees comes from corporate donors. In the 1994 election cycle, corporations alone donated $50.1 million in soft money, which represented almost 53 percent of party soft money receipts. By 1998, this sum had grown to more than $92 million, or about 52 percent of all soft money donations. Other business organizations, including individual incorporated entities and trade associations, gave an additional $5.9 million in 1994 and $13.5 million in 1998. Business sources were thus responsible for $55.9 million in soft money gifts in 1994 and $105.7 million in gifts in 1998, or about 60 percent of the total soft money donations in each of these cycles.[4]

Similarly, a 1997 analysis conducted by the *Los Angeles Times* of the political donations made by the 544 biggest public and private companies revealed that soft money donations by these corporations had more than tripled between 1992 and 1996, growing from $16 million to $51 million. In comparison, the contributions made by the PACs maintained by these committees rose only from $43 million to $52 million.[5]

The sums attributable to business interests are even larger if the donations made by business executives are included with the amounts given from their companies' corporate treasuries. For example, a Center for Responsive Politics study found that businesses and their executives or employees gave a total of about $172 million in soft money in 1996, as compared to $66 million in 1992. Of this $172 million, approximately $95 million went to the Republican party and $77 million went to Democrats.[6]

As for labor money, the Center for Responsive Politics study found that labor unions and their executives gave $4.2 million in soft money in 1992 and more than twice as much, $9.9 million, in 1996. Labor sources thus provided a relatively minor sum to party committees when compared to corporate giving. Most of this money, approximately $9.3 million, went to the Democrats. The Campaign Reform Project also examined labor donations and determined that labor organizations gave $4.7 million in 1994 and $7.8 million in 1998. Labor contributions were thus responsible for less than 5 percent of the soft money donated in each of these election cycles. Viewed from another perspective, labor groups give only $1 to the party committees for every $10 given by corporations.

The largest soft money donors tend to be companies or industries that are heavily regulated by the federal government or those whose profits can be dramatically affected by prospective government regulations. For example, according to an analysis of 1996 donors conducted by the Center for Responsive Politics, extraordinary amounts of soft money were donated by industries that would be affected by pending legislation.[7]

- Tobacco companies and their executives, who have faced concerted federal efforts to strengthen the regulations governing tobacco sales and advertising, as well as the possibility of congressional action to settle ongoing lawsuits, gave a total of $6.83 million in 1996, with $5.77 million donated to the Republicans and $1.06 million to the Democrats. This group was led by Philip Morris, which donated the most soft money of all contributors in 1996, giving a total of about $3 million, $2.52 million of which went to the Republicans. RJR Nabisco gave a total of $1.44 million, with $1.18 million going to the Republicans.

- Telecommunications companies, in the midst of deregulation and interested in an array of proposals that will affect the industry, contributed $6.28 million in soft money, almost equally divided between Democrats ($3.2 million) and Republicans ($3.1 million). The leader in this group was the communications giant AT&T, which gave about $552,000 to Republicans and $422,000 to Democrats, for a total of $974,000; one of its major competitors, MCI Telecommunications, gave $964,000, with almost two-thirds of that amount, $607,000, going to the Democrats. NYNEX, one of the regional telephone companies, gave $651,000, $411,000 of which went to the Republicans.

- The oil and gas industry, which is affected by a wide range of federal laws and environmental regulations, gave $9.13 million in soft money, $6.59 million of which went to the Republicans, $2.54 million to the Democrats. Atlantic Richfield and its executives, the leading donor in this group, gave a total of $1.25 million, with $764,000 sent to Republican committees and $486,000 to Democratic committees.

These examples, while noteworthy, are not atypical of soft money contributions. Most of the largest corporate donations come from companies or industries with a stake in federal policymaking, and many split their contributions between the two parties in hope of gaining access to legislators on both sides of the aisle.

How Much Do Parties Spend to Assist Federal Candidates?

Parties spend a relatively small share of their budgets on direct assistance to federal candidates, which is an activity that must be financed with hard money. Approximately 40 to 50 percent of the monies raised by national party committees are used to pay staff salaries, administrative costs, fundraising expenses, loan repayments, and other overhead.[8] Direct assistance to candidates, in the form of either direct contributions or coordinated expenditures, typically averages about 10 to 15 percent.

Since 1986, the Democrats have allocated an average of about 13 percent of their total federal spending to coordinated spending. The Republicans, who in recent elections have raised about twice as much federal money as the Democrats, have disbursed about 9 percent of their total federal spending in a coordinated manner. From 1990 to 1996, the Democratic and Republican parties each spent at least $20 million to $30 million per election on coordinated expenditures. This represented a substantial increase from the levels of the early 1980s. By contrast, the major parties spend only 1 to 2 percent of their federal funds on direct contributions to candidates, or an average in recent elections of $2 million to $3.5 million per election.[9] (See Table 6.2.)

WHO RECEIVES PARTY FUNDING?

In allocating their resources, the national party committees have the same basic objective: to win the White House and Congress, or at least to maximize the number of seats their party holds in Congress. Accordingly, they tend to focus on candidates in close contests or in marginal districts where party assistance might make a difference in whether the party candidate wins or loses the election.

Overall, Democratic party committees disbursed more than $22 million on coordinated expenditures in the 1996 election cycle, as compared to more than $30 million for the Republicans. In both parties in 1996, the majority of party-coordinated expenditures were made on behalf of nonincumbents. The Democrats devoted 85 percent of their total coordinated expenditures in Senate races to challengers (31 percent) and open-seat candidates (54 percent). In House races, 80 percent was spent on behalf of nonincumbents, with challengers (56 percent) receiving more than twice the share that went to open-seat candidates (24 percent). Almost all of the money spent on behalf of incumbents—15 percent in Senate races and 20 percent in House races— went to incumbents who were in jeopardy of losing their seats.

The Republicans' coordinated activity also favored nonincumbents. The Republican committees, however, spent more than the Democrats to defend incumbents because an unusually large number of them were involved in close races, especially among the large freshman class in the House, most of whom won in 1994 with 55 percent of the vote or less. Even with this unusually large number of threatened incumbents, the Senate and House committees

Table 6.2
Political Party Federal Financial Activity,
1978–98 ($ Millions)

	Election Cycle										
	1978	1980	1982	1984	1986	1988	1990	1992	1994	1996	1998
Democrats											
Raised	26.4	37.2	39.3	98.5	64.8	127.9	85.7	177.7	139.1	221.6	160.0
Spent	26.9	35.0	40.1	97.4	65.9	121.9	90.9	171.9	137.8	214.3	155.3
Contributed	1.8	1.7	1.7	2.6	1.7	1.7	1.5	1.9	2.2	2.2	1.2
Coord. Exp.	0.4	4.9	3.3	9.0	9.0	17.9	8.7	28.0	21.1	22.6	18.6
Indep. Exp.	—	—	—	—	—	—	—	—	—	1.5	1.5
Republicans											
Raised	84.5	169.5	215.0	297.9	255.2	263.3	206.3	267.3	245.6	416.5	285.0
Spent	85.9	161.8	214.0	300.8	258.9	257.0	213.5	256.1	234.7	408.5	275.9
Contributed	4.5	4.5	5.6	4.9	3.4	3.4	2.9	3.0	2.8	3.7	2.6
Coord. Exp.	4.3	12.4	14.3	20.1	14.3	22.7	10.7	33.8	20.4	31.0	15.7
Indep. Exp.	—	—	—	—	—	—	—	—	—	10.0	0.3

Source: Based on the Federal Election Commission reports on political party activity for 1995–96 and 1997–98.

each disbursed close to two-thirds of their coordinated funds on races involv-
ing nonincumbents. In Senate races, 63 percent of coordinated expenditures
were made on behalf of nonincumbents, with challengers receiving 21 percent
of the total amount expended and open-seat candidates receiving 42 percent.
In the House elections, where 63 percent of the funds also went to nonincumbents, challengers received 34 percent of the coordinated money, while
open-seat candidates received 29 percent.

These 1996 allocations are similar to those in previous cycles. That most
of the monies spent in coordination with candidates are targeted on nonincumbents and close races makes sense, given the purpose these party funds
serve in the electoral process. Party committees rely on their coordinated expenditures to help their marginal candidates or viable challengers win elections.

WHAT EFFECT HAVE RECENT COURT RULINGS HAD ON PARTY SPENDING?

One reason why parties spend relatively small shares of their budgets directly
assisting their candidates for federal office is that the FECA restricts the
amounts a party committee may contribute to a federal candidate or spend
on a candidate's behalf. A national party committee may give no more than
$5,000 per election to a House candidate and no more than $17,500 total to
a Senate candidate. Coordinated expenditures also are limited, and the current
ceilings provide modest levels of funding given the actual cost of campaign services. For example, the 1998 limit of $32,550 in a House race was not enough
to pay for the cost of sending one letter to each eligible voter in a congressional
district.

Unlike other spending limits, the party-coordinated spending limits were
not specifically challenged in the *Buckley* case, so they have continued to be
part of the law. These restrictions are now being challenged in the case of
Colorado Republican Federal Campaign Committee v. Federal Election Commission.
This case was initially heard by the Supreme Court in 1996, when the Court
decided that the monies spent by the Colorado Republican party on certain
radio advertisements in 1986 did not count against the party's coordinated
spending limit.[10] In a splintered decision, the Court ruled that the expenditures
were not coordinated with a candidate and thus were not subject to the party's
coordinated spending limit. Further, a majority of the justices affirmed the
right of party organizations to make unlimited independent expenditures in
support of a federal candidate. But the Court was divided on the question of
whether limits on coordinated spending were constitutional. This question
was remanded to the district court for specific argument.

The immediate effect of the *Colorado* ruling was to provide party committees with a means of giving unlimited assistance to their candidates through independent expenditures. "Independent expenditures" are a particular form of campaign finance under the provisions of the FECA. An independent expenditure, in this context, is any money spent expressly to advocate the election or defeat of a federal candidate that is disbursed without any coordination with a candidate or campaign committee. Such expenditures are usually made by PACs or other political groups as a means of supplementing any contributions they might make to federal candidates. These organizations have at times found this approach to be a more effective means of helping a favored candidate than a simple donation because, unlike contributions, independent expenditures are not subject to any limits, although they must be financed through monies raised under the relevant contribution limits of federal law.

Prior to 1996, federal regulations assumed that parties could not make independent expenditures. The presumption was that parties and the candidates who run on their labels are intimately connected, and it was illogical to speak of a party organization as being "independent" of its presidential nominee or one of its other candidates for federal office. Instead, federal law recognized the relationship between parties and candidates, and thus allowed parties to spend additional monies on behalf of their candidates in the form of limited coordinated expenditures.

In the summer of 1996, in the aftermath of the *Colorado* ruling, both parties established separate operations to spend monies independently, disbursing a total of more than $11 million in the weeks before the general election. Most of this amount, $9.7 million, was spent by the National Republican Senatorial Committee, which made independent expenditures in nineteen of the thirty-four Senate contests. The committee spent about $4.5 million in support of its candidates, and $5.2 million against Democratic opponents. The Democratic Senatorial Campaign Committee began later than its Republican counterpart and spent $1.4 million in seven Senate races. Of this amount, $1.3 million was spent against Republican opponents and only $45,000 on behalf of Democrats.[11]

In 1998, party committees once again made independent expenditures in connection with federal elections, but the amounts expended were well below those of 1996. In all, the parties allocated only $1.8 million to independent expenditures, $1.5 million of which was spent by the Democrats. Most of the Democratic expenditures were made by the DSCC, with $529,000 spent in support of candidates in open-seat races and $800,000 spent against Republican challengers and open-seat candidates. Independent expenditures also were made by some state and local committees, including more than $131,000 in disbursements in support of Democratic senate candidates. Republican committees made only about $300,000 in independent expenditures, including $236,000 in disbursements made on behalf of Senate candidates by the NRSC and $41,000 against Democratic candidates in House open-seat races by Republican state and local committees.[12]

Whether the decline in independent spending by party committees in 1998 is a precursor of future financial strategies remains to be seen. While the option to spend monies independently gives parties the freedom to disburse unlimited sums in support of a candidate, it also imposes certain burdens and costs on party organizations. Because independent expenditures expressly advocate the election or defeat of a federal candidate, they must be financed with hard money. Second, this approach may require a separate administrative or financial structure in order to ensure that there is no coordination between a candidate and the party organ making the independent expenditures. Such a structure makes this option more costly than a program of coordinated spending. Further, it requires a party committee to act independently of its candidates, which may limit the party in its other activities (for example, it may not be able to make coordinated expenditures on a candidate's behalf), and may result in the party intervening in a race in a way that does not meet with the candidate's approval.

HOW DO PARTY COMMITTEES SPEND SOFT MONEY?

In general, the national party committees spend soft money on four broad kinds of political activity: (1) joint federal and nonfederal activities, which include such items as administrative costs incurred for shared federal and nonfederal political activity, costs of fundraising efforts that generate hard and soft money, and voter registration and mobilization drives that benefit federal and nonfederal candidates; (2) direct financial transfers to state and local parties; (3) direct contributions to state and local candidates; and (4) miscellaneous expenses, including such items as building funds (money to construct buildings or refurbish offices) and other non-campaign-related expenditures.

In 1998, Republican party committees spent $127.7 million in soft money. Of this amount, $49.3 million was allocated to joint activities, $34.3 million was transferred to state party committees, and $11.1 million was contributed to state and local candidates. The remaining sum, about $41 million, was spent for a variety of other purposes. The Democratic committees disbursed about $93 million in soft money, with almost half of this total, $43.2 million, expended on joint activities. The Democrats transferred about $34.8 million to state party committees, made about $3.8 million in contributions to state and local candidates, and disbursed $18.2 million for other purposes.[13]

Beyond these broad generalizations, it is difficult to itemize the use of soft money funds. One of the problems with soft money is that, even though the FEC has required the national party committees to disclose their soft money funds since 1991, the regulations require only broad categorization with respect to the purpose of any expenditure. Nor do parties have to report the purposes of any monies transferred to state and local party organizations. Itemized disclosure of the use of these funds is left to the respective state parties, subject to state disclosure laws, which are generally less effective than federal requirements.

A significant portion of the soft money spent on joint activities is used to pay the nonfederal share of administrative expenses and fundraising costs. Another major share is used to identify party voters and turn them out to vote. Because voter turnout efforts affect both federal and nonfederal elections (those who do vote usually vote for candidates up and down the ticket), they are financed as joint activities. Under the allocation rules established by the FEC in 1991, these voter contact efforts financed by the national party committees must be paid for with a mix of hard and soft money—in presidential election years, the mix is a minimum of 65 percent hard money and 35 percent soft money; in nonpresidential years, the mix is a minimum of 60 percent hard money and 40 percent soft money. So for every $100 spent on voter turnout efforts in 1996, the national parties were required to use $65 in hard money and $35 in soft money.

The Democratic national committees spent roughly $40 million on party building and voter mobilization programs in 1996, according to one major analysis.[14] This includes the hard and soft money used to purchase voter lists, finance direct mail expenses, and set up telephone banks. If 35 percent of this amount represented soft money, the total would be $14 million, or slightly less than half of the total soft money spent on joint activities. The Democrats also spent about $5 million on generic party advertisements designed to mobilize ethnic and racial minorities and gave a few hundred thousand dollars to three different groups to help get minority voters to the polls.

The Republicans spent $48.3 million on their voter mobilization programs. The Republican National Committee (RNC) transferred $15.3 million to state party committees for grassroots activities. These committees spent an additional $33 million. The RNC also gave $4.6 million in soft money to Americans for Tax Reform, an antitax group, and $1.4 million to a few right-to-life groups and conservative organizations, for voter education and mobilization efforts.[15]

The most notable change in soft money spending in 1996 was in the amounts of money transferred to state and local committees. In all, the Republicans transferred almost ten times more money to states in 1996 than they did in 1992; the Democrats transferred seven times more than their total in 1992. Of the $271 million in soft money spent by the national party committees in 1996, almost $115 million was sent to state committees. In 1998, the national parties transferred about $64 million to the states, or more than a quarter of the $220 million they disbursed from soft money accounts.

One reason for such transfers was that many state committees lacked the resources needed to implement party plans, so the national committees provided the funds. The primary reason for the change in strategy, however, was that state parties can usually spend more soft money on joint activities than can national party committees. The FEC regulations establish a different allocation formula for state party expenditures than that applied to national party spending. Under the rules, the proportion of soft money that can be used by state committees is based on a ratio of federal races to nonfederal races on a state's ballot.[16] As a result, most states have more nonfederal than federal offices on the ballot, so they can use a larger share of soft money than that allowed the national committees. So by shifting the money to states and then having the state parties pay for any expenses, more soft money can be used than would be the case if the national parties paid the bills. Finally, by shifting the monies to the states, the national committees can effectively avoid meaningful disclosure since many states lack effective disclosure laws.

WHY IS SOFT MONEY SO CONTROVERSIAL?

Soft money is antithetical to the regulatory regime established by the FECA. It has undermined the efficacy of contribution limits by providing individuals with a way to make contributions in excess of federal limits. It has allowed party organizations to raise money from sources that have long been prohibited from making contributions in connection with federal elections. And it has undermined the presidential public financing scheme by providing parties with a means of raising unlimited sums and using it for purposes, such as voter identification and mobilization, that can directly benefit a presidential nominee.

As parties have placed a greater and greater emphasis on soft money, they have increasingly enlisted the support of federal officeholders and candidates to help raise these funds. The president, vice president, major party leaders, and other elected officials are often the featured guest at soft money fundraisers, primarily because the parties have found that the best way to raise these large donations is to offer the donors access to elected officials and candidates. In addition, party leaders are increasingly responsible for directly soliciting large soft money gifts for the party committees, spending hours on the telephone asking for contributions, meeting with donors personally, or traveling throughout the country to attend major donor fundraising events. In 2000, the congressional leadership in each of the major parties assumed a particularly visible role in soft money fundraising, including the personal solicitation of donors targeted for inclusion in the "clubs" or "teams" that have been established by the congressional campaign committees for donors of $100,000 or more.[17]

Moreover, some candidates for federal office are now establishing "joint fundraising committees" or "victory funds" with party organizations that are designed to raise money for both a candidate and the party committee that will assist the candidate in the election. These committees raise both hard and soft dollars, thus providing federal candidates with a means of raising soft money that will be used for their campaigns.[18] But the funds are not deposited in the candidates' campaign committee accounts since that would be illegal under federal law. Instead, the funds are retained in these joint fundraising committees or eventually transferred to the appropriate party committee bank account. This tactic keeps the transaction legal but does not obscure the fact that more and more candidates are now involved in the solicitation of contributions that would be considered illegal if given directly to their campaigns.

In these ways, soft money fundraising encourages the types of relations between large donors and policymakers that can undermine public confidence in the process and raise the potential for abuse. Instead of shielding candidates from large donors, the parties have encouraged greater access to candidates, which raises the issue of whether such access provides these donors with undue influence in the legislative process or creates the types of appearance of corruption that the campaign finance system is supposed to discourage. While some experts contend that such access is not a cause for great concern, most critics of soft money claim that it is the primary reason why soft money fundraising needs to be reformed.

The most highly publicized example of such access to the president and White House was that provided to the Democratic party's major donors through White House coffees, special events, and Lincoln Bedroom stays conducted throughout 1996. Although no money changed hands at these events, those who attended the coffees contributed more than $25 million to the Democrats and sent a signal to the public that the White House was open to those who could pay "the price of admission."

International oil financier Roger Tamraz epitomized the problem of soft money in the eyes of many advocates of reform. Tamraz, who was eventually called to testify before the Senate Governmental Affairs Committee as part of its investigation into campaign fundraising, had a plan to construct an oil pipeline across the Caspian Sea, but in order to undertake this project, he needed the backing of the United States. He hoped to get access to plead his case to the president by donating at least $177,000 in soft money to the Democrats. Although an official at the National Security Council advised against giving Tamraz access to the White House, DNC officials and others lobbied on his behalf, and he was eventually invited to six functions at the White House. At a March 27, 1996, dinner he had an opportunity to tell the president about the pipeline project. Tamraz did not receive backing for his project. But he freely admitted to the Senate committee that he had made his contributions in order to buy access, and he declared in response to a question that "I think next time I will give $600,000."[19]

The Republicans also have offered donors privileged access to elected officials in exchange for contributions. One RNC fundraising program, known as "Team 100," offered membership to donors at a price of $100,000 to join, $100,000 every fourth year thereafter, and $25,000 in each of the years in between. Members are given the opportunity to attend national and regional meetings with the Republican leadership and elected officials, participate in international Team 100 business missions, and attend special party events, including the national nominating convention.[20] Another program, known as the Senatorial Trust, requires an annual contribution of $10,000 in personal funds or $15,000 in corporate funds and provides members with "the unique opportunity to participate in quarterly meetings with Republican Senators, candidates and other national VIPs. These meetings are private forums dedicated to discussing specific issues and addressing important national concerns. . . ."[21]

Common Cause, among others, argues that corporations and industries that give millions of dollars to the parties often realize billions of dollars in benefits from federal policy decisions. For example, in July 1997, tobacco industry allies slipped a provision into the budget reconciliation bill that would have effectively given tobacco companies a $50 billion tax break. This one-sentence provision, which would have allowed tobacco companies to use the revenues raised by a new cigarette tax to pay their obligations under a proposed tobacco settlement, appeared without discussion or debate in a conference report. When the tax break was revealed, it became a matter of such controversy that the Congress was forced to rescind it in September.[22]

Another provision of the budget bill involved a revision in tax rules that was heavily supported by the oil and gas industry, another major soft money donor. The revision relaxed the rules on the alternative minimum tax, thereby reducing the amount of taxes these companies had to pay. Another change involved a cut in the capital gains tax, which was heavily supported by the securities industry. Securities companies gave a total of $10.5 million to Republicans and $7 million to Democrats.[23]

While advocates of soft money reform offer strong arguments for eliminating this form of finance, the debate over soft money is complicated by issues that have been raised as to whether the federal government can regulate this practice. Some observers have noted that parties raise this money for use in nonfederal elections and that the parties have a right to raise monies allowable under state laws for use in those states. So if Virginia allows corporate contributions in its state elections, as it does, then the national parties should be allowed to raise corporate funds for use in Virginia's elections. In this view, to adopt a federal law that prevents national committees from raising and spending soft money would be a violation of the principle of federalism because it would undermine the right of states and localities to determine their own election laws.[24] Most advocates of reform, however, contend that effective regulation of campaign finance can be achieved only by regulating soft money.

7

ISSUE ADVOCACY

Federal courts have made a distinction between two basic types of political speech: express advocacy and issue advocacy. In simplest terms, express advocacy is any communication that advocates the election or defeat of a federal candidate; issue advocacy is any communication that does not. Issue advocacy therefore covers three distinct types of political speech: speech that advocates positions on issues, provides information about issues, and provides information about candidates. Issue advocacy includes communications about a candidate's voting record or position on an issue, advertisements that encourage candidates to take a position on a policy proposal, or communications that seek to educate the public about an issue or policy.

HOW IS ISSUE ADVOCACY DISTINGUISHED FROM EXPRESS ADVOCACY?

Although the distinction between express advocacy and issue advocacy is easy to state, deciding how to distinguish these two categories of speech has become a matter of contentious debate. This distinction is important because, as noted in Chapter 2, in its 1976 *Buckley* decision, the Supreme Court limited the scope of the FECA's regulatory authority to express advocacy, arguing that the law's original purpose—to regulate all expenditures made for the purpose of influencing a federal election—was too broad. The Court held that the restrictions of federal law were limited to speech that contained explicit words of advocacy of election or defeat. To explain and illustrate this concept, the Court suggested in a footnote that express advocacy would include communications that contain such words as "vote for," "elect," "support," "cast your ballot for," "Smith for Congress," "vote against," "defeat," or "reject."[1] As will be explained in greater detail in this chapter, messages that did not contain such language could be considered issue advocacy and were thus exempt from federal regulation.

HOW HAVE COURTS DISTINGUISHED ISSUE ADVOCACY IN THE AFTERMATH OF *BUCKLEY*?

In searching for a test that would draw a clear line between the two types of political speech, most court decisions issued since 1976 have embraced the words suggested in the footnote in *Buckley* as the standard for determining the difference. These courts have held that so long as a message or advertisement does not contain these particular words, it should not be considered express advocacy and should not be subject to federal regulation. Consequently, the *Buckley* examples are now commonly referred to as "the magic words." The First, Second, and Fourth Circuit Courts have all adopted this approach.[2]

Other legal authorities, including the FEC and Ninth Circuit Court, have argued that it is not enough simply to look at the words in a message. Instead, they argue that because candidates are closely linked to issues and policies, and because the broadcast of a candidate's voting record or information about an issue can be a means of encouraging public support for one candidate over another, it is important to look at the broader context of a message to determine whether it presents an "electioneering message" that is clearly intended to encourage the audience to support or oppose a particular candidate for federal office. This is the general approach adopted by the Ninth Circuit Court in *Federal Election Commission* v. *Furgatch*. In this case, the court ruled that speech without the "magic words" could amount to express advocacy if, when "read as a whole, and with limited reference to external events," a message is susceptible to no other reasonable interpretation than that it is "an exhortation to vote for or against a specific candidate."[3]

Following the *Furgatch* decision, the FEC in 1995 promulgated new regulations to define the types of communication that constitute express advocacy.[4] But these rules were challenged successfully in the First District, where the court decided that the regulations were unconstitutional because they moved beyond the "magic words" test affirmed in *Buckley* and other decisions.[5] The FEC, however, continues to argue for more stringent regulation of issue advocacy spending.

WHY HAS ISSUE ADVOCACY ADVERTISING BECOME SO PROMINENT IN RECENT ELECTIONS?

Issue advocacy is not a new form of political spending. Interest groups and party organizations have traditionally informed the public about issues and candidates' voting records by distributing leaflets, mailing information to their members, rating the candidates based on their voting records, and conducting public advertising campaigns. Such information is a valuable and essential component of any election and helps ensure that voters have access to a wide variety of information and perspectives when deciding whom to support on Election Day.

In 1994, the DNC conducted an advertising campaign in support of the president's health care plan, and early in the fall of 1995 the Republicans broadcast radio ads advocating their position on federal budget issues. The controversy started later in 1995, when the DNC and Democratic state party committees began running ads on the president's budget agenda and his administration's accomplishments. Some of President Clinton's campaign advisers wanted to stage an advertising blitz to bolster Clinton's popularity heading into the election year. But they faced the problem of how to conduct such an effort yet remain within the FECA's presidential campaign spending limits. The solution was to have the DNC and state party committees finance issue ads that would promote the president's agenda and accomplishments. The DNC began televising ads in October 1995 and thus became the first party committee in the 1996 election cycle to finance issue ads to help a candidate.

The DNC issue ads were designed to promote the president's accomplishments and to position the Republican-controlled Congress as a group of conservative extremists who advocated positions that favored the wealthy. The ads were financed with a combination of hard and soft monies in accordance with federal party allocation formulas. By January 1, 1996, the committee had aired ads in 42 percent of the nation's media markets at an estimated cost of $18 million. By the end of June, according to estimates by Common Cause, the DNC and state party committees had spent an estimated $34 million on pro-Clinton advertising, with $22 million of this amount coming from soft money and $12 million from hard money. Most of this spending was focused on twelve general election battleground states that would be essential to Clinton's reelection prospects. Additional ads throughout the election cycle brought total spending to an estimated $44 million.[6]

The DNC advertising effort proved to be the harbinger of a new approach to election campaigning. Instead of focusing solely on direct contributions, independent expenditures, and, in the case of parties, coordinated expenditures, all of which must be financed with hard money, interest groups and party organizations began to spend money on issue ads designed to influence the outcome of federal elections. This new approach allowed them to use funds not regulated by the FECA in a way that benefited specific federal candidates. They simply had to ensure that any communications financed in this manner did not include the "magic words" used to define express advocacy. Groups therefore began to broadcast ads that asked voters to call an elected official, write for more information, or urge a candidate to support or renounce a given policy position. Some ads did not even make any suggestions about what actions to take; they simply presented information about a candidate's views or voting record. So by abiding by certain legal technicalities, parties could use soft money on communications that presented themes and information similar to those that appear in express advocacy messages. Interest groups could avoid federal regulation altogether since their issue advocacy communications are not subject to the party allocations formulas or disclosure rules.

The AFL-CIO embarked on an ambitious issue advocacy campaign early in 1996. This advertising was particularly targeted at vulnerable Republican members of Congress, especially first-term members. In all, the labor group spent more than $20 million on issue ads in at least forty-four congressional districts, including thirty-two represented by Republican House freshmen. Most of this spending was done in two waves of advertising, one timed to coincide with primary elections and the other in the first three weeks of October. In the districts where the AFL-CIO advertised, the Republicans won twenty-nine and the Democrats won fifteen.[7]

The RNC waited until late March, when Senator Robert Dole clinched the party's presidential nomination, to launch its own issue advocacy campaign. The purpose of this campaign, according to then–RNC chairman Haley Barbour, was "to show the differences between Dole and Clinton and between Republicans and Democrats on the issues facing our country, so we can engage full-time in one of the most consequential elections in our history."[8] Between March and its August national convention, the RNC spent approximately $20 million on issue ads. In April, the ads focused on Clinton's record on welfare and taxes. In May, one ad attacked Clinton's record on gasoline taxes, and $3 million was spent on an ad that focused on Dole's biography and mentioned legislative issues. A July ad attacked Clinton's failure to deliver a tax cut to the middle class, while one in August criticized the president's stance on drugs.[9]

The Republican House and Senate campaign committees sponsored issue ads that supplemented the RNC's efforts. The National Republican Senatorial Committee spent about $2 million to televise issue ads in five states. The

National Republican Congressional Committee spent approximately $27 million to televise six different ads in competitive districts.

The Democratic Hill committees also sponsored general election issue ads. The Democratic Senate Campaign Committee transferred $10 million to the fourteen states where the closest Senate races were being contested. The Democratic Congressional Campaign Committee transferred $8.5 million to Democratic state committees to help finance ads that aired in the districts of sixty marginal House members, most of whom were first-term Republicans.

In addition to the parties and labor organizations, at least two dozen other groups engaged in issue advocacy spending, particularly television and radio advertising, during the 1996 general election campaign. For example, the Sierra Club, one of the nation's leading environmental groups, engaged in a $3 million issue advocacy campaign that included a $1 million radio and television advertising blitz aimed at more than two dozen members of Congress. The organization also spent $3.5 million on 2 million voter guides that presented the environmental records of particular federal candidates. In the 1994 election cycle, the group had spent only $100,000 on issue advocacy.[10]

The U.S. Chamber of Commerce led the formation of a coalition of thirty-two business groups, known simply as "The Coalition," which spent an estimated $5 million on issue ads, in addition to mailing 2 million letters to its members.[11] Citizens for the Republic Education Fund, a tax-exempt organization founded by Ronald Reagan's former political director, Lyn Nofziger, spent more than $4 million on issue ads to help Republican Senate candidates and House candidates in more than a dozen congressional districts.[12] The right-wing Christian Coalition spent a reported $10 million to print and distribute 46 million voter guides. The organization also broadcast radio ads and conducted extensive get-out-the-vote campaigns.[13]

According to one analysis, 87 percent of the televised issue advocacy ads referred to a federal officeholder or candidate, and 59 percent included a picture of a federal officeholder or candidate.[14] While the groups or individuals sponsoring the ads claimed that they were "issue ads," most election observers and journalists judged them to be thinly veiled campaign ads, which had been cleverly scripted to avoid the words that indicate express advocacy.

The 1996 elections thus established a new model for election campaigning that became an established practice in 1998. According to an analysis by the Annenberg Public Policy Center, seventy-seven organizations broadcast issue ads in 1997 and 1998, as compared to twenty-seven organizations in the 1996 election cycle. Most of these ads were broadcast during the election year. Approximately 80 percent of the ads broadcast during the general election period named a specific candidate, and more than half (51.5 percent) contained messages that were designed to attack a candidate's views or position on an issue.[15]

As in 1996, the national party committees were the largest issue advertisers. But unlike 1996, the parties waited until the general election period to
broadcast most of their ads in hopes of having a greater effect on the outcomes of key races. According to the Annenberg study, almost 71 percent of
the issue ads aired after September 1 were produced by the Democratic and
Republican party committees, as compared to about 10 percent of the ads
broadcast earlier in the election cycle. About 60 percent of these ads attacked
the position of a candidate of the opposing party. Accordingly, the study concluded that "the data show that party issue ads were used in the final phases of
the campaign to attack, leaving candidates to take the higher road of self-
advocacy and comparison."[16]

Most of the monies spent on issue advocacy were expended by Republican
party committees. The cornerstone of this effort was a plan designated
"Operation Breakout," which was designed to spend $37 million on issue advo-
cacy advertising during the last two months of the campaign. As much as $20
million of this amount was raised by Republican House members, with the
balance drawn from party soft money accounts. In all, the effort resulted in the
production of more than fifty television ads, with ads broadcast in thirty-four
states. In addition, the NRCC launched a much-publicized $10 million adver-
tising effort during the last week of the campaign, which revolved around
three television ads aired in selected markets that highlighted themes or issues
related to the Monica Lewinsky scandal. The NRSC also financed a reported
$5 million in issue advocacy advertising as part of an estimated $9 million in
expenditures made on behalf of Republican Senate candidates.[17]

The DNC and its affiliates were not as forthcoming as their Republican
counterparts in their public discussions of their issue advertising strategy, so less
detailed information as to the extent of their efforts is known. In general, the
Democrats spent less than the Republicans on efforts such as these, in large
part because they were facing competing financial pressures created by a $15
million debt and more than $12 million in legal bills related to the 1996 cam-
paign finance investigations.[18] According to the Annenberg compilation, the
DSCC spent roughly $8 million on issue advertising and the DCCC about
$7 million during the late phases of the campaign.

HOW MUCH IS SPENT ON
ISSUE ADVOCACY ADVERTISING?

Because there is no federal disclosure requirement for issue advocacy advertising by groups and organizations, and because party committees do not have
to itemize their issue ad disbursements, it is impossible to determine from FEC

records exactly how much money is spent in this manner. The best available estimate of total 1996 issue advocacy advertising expenditures is the figure developed by the Annenberg Public Policy Center, which surveyed a wide range of sources and newspaper reports on more than two dozen groups or organizations that sponsored ads during the 1996 cycle. According to this analysis, these groups and party committees spent an estimated $135 million to $150 million.[19] This figure probably understates the scope of such spending, since it includes only those groups willing to discuss their spending, does not include the Christian Coalition, and underestimates the amounts spent by the party committees and the Citizens for the Republic Education Fund.

The Annenberg Public Policy Center's 1998 survey of issue advocacy advertising estimated total spending at $275 million to $340 million, or more than twice the amount expended in the 1996 cycle.[20] But this estimate included advertisements, such as those sponsored by the tobacco companies in 1997 during the legislative debate on tobacco regulation and the settlement of legal claims, that were not conducted in proximity to an election or designed to influence the outcome of a pending election. As such, they were "true" issue ads, not the surrogate campaign ads that have been the focus of recent controversy.

While it is difficult to determine the extent of issue advocacy spending, it is impossible to determine the sources of the funding. While the national party committees must disclose their hard and soft money receipts, the funds used to pay for issue ads cannot be accurately determined from the reports. Nonparty committees or groups are under no federal obligation to disclose either their funding or expenditures for issue advocacy since this activity is not considered to be a federal election activity under the law. Even those groups that willingly report their issue ad spending are usually unwilling to disclose the sources of their funding. Consequently, very little is known about where the money comes from, who the largest donors are, or who supports different groups.

WHY IS ISSUE ADVOCACY ADVERTISING SO CONTROVERSIAL?

In the eyes of most advocates of reform, issue advocacy allows parties and organized interests to circumvent the restrictions of federal campaign finance law and to finance political activity designed to influence federal elections without being subject to public scrutiny. The growth of issue advocacy spending is thus seen as a loophole in federal law that needs to be closed if federal regulations are to be effective.

Issue advocacy advertising also is controversial because it is not subject to public disclosure. The organized groups that engage in such advocacy often have such generic names as "Citizens for Reform," "Citizens for a Sound Economy," "The Coalition," and "Women for Tax Reform." Consequently, the name of the group sponsoring a particular ad, which must be disclosed in broadcast advertisements, often does not provide viewers with information that can help them assess the source of the information being presented. This type of spending thus undermines the notion of a well-informed electorate, and increases the risk of corruption since the sources of funding for these efforts are not subject to public scrutiny.

Proponents of reform also are concerned about the effects of issue advocacy on the conduct of campaigns and candidate behavior. This problem was highlighted in a recent study of issue advocacy spending in 1998, which concluded: "With the growth in non-candidate campaign activity by parties and groups, candidates may still be held responsible for attacks on their opponents, but in fact may have no control over them. On the other hand, candidates can benefit from this system by claiming the high ground while their party or other friendly groups slam their opponents."[21]

Those who oppose any reform of the rules governing issue advocacy counter these claims by noting that issue speech is strictly protected by the First Amendment and is essential to a healthy democracy. They consider the recent growth in issue advocacy to be a beneficial development. Such advertising makes a valuable contribution to civic life by providing more information to the electorate, encouraging policy discussion, and promoting the type of free and robust political debate that is the hallmark of our political system. It can raise topics that candidates might choose to neglect, force candidates to defend aspects of their records that they might otherwise try to avoid, and disrupt a candidate's attempt to control the debate that takes place in an election campaign.[22]

Opponents of reform further argue that additional regulation would have a chilling effect on political speech. A more stringent standard might subject groups or nonprofit organizations to additional reporting requirements and funding limitations (for example, ads might have to be financed with regulated money rather than unrestricted funds), which in turn might serve to discourage them from engaging in this form of speech. Moreover, the adoption of a standard such as that suggested by the court in *Furgatch* would require regulators to examine the context of an ad and the speaker's motivation. This would not only pose a risk of chilling speech, but it would also lead to a greater role for the courts in resolving political debates.[23]

Given these varying perspectives, and the First Amendment considerations that have spurred the growth of issue advocacy, it is not surprising that it has become one of the fundamental issues in the current campaign finance reform debate. It is a particularly difficult and perplexing issue because elections are not bounded institutions; that is, it is often not possible to separate speech made about an issue in connection with an election from speech made in connection with the legislative process or general education of the electorate. For example, Congress is often in session during the weeks before an election. An ad that might be designed to encourage a member to support a particular bill might also have the effect of influencing voters to support or oppose that member. Conversely, an ad that solely discusses a policy issue might make that issue more salient to voters and thus affect their voting decisions. How to draw a clear line separating speech that should be regulated from that which should not is an issue that is difficult to resolve.

Early in the 2000 election cycle, the controversy over issue advocacy spending took on a new dimension as a result of yet another innovation in campaign finance practices. This new tactic involved the establishment of political committees under Section 527 of the Internal Revenue Code. Section 527 of the tax code exempts "political organizations" from income taxes. This exemption was originally intended to cover political party committees, candidate committees, and state and federal political committees that are registered and report to the FEC. But recent changes in Internal Revenue Service (IRS) advice and federal court rulings made it possible for Section 527 groups to engage in political activity without having to register either with the FEC or with state campaign finance authorities. So long as a Section 527 organization does not "expressly advocate" the election or defeat of federal candidates, it can engage in activities that seek to "influence the outcome of federal elections" without being subject to FECA restrictions or disclosure requirements. Moreover, because these organizations are exempt from federal taxation, they can receive gifts of more than $10,000 without being subject to the federal gift tax.[24]

Section 527 was established before issue advocacy advertising became a popular campaign strategy. This provision therefore did not require the disclosure of an organization's contributors, because Congress assumed that they would already be reported to the FEC or the appropriate state agency. This gap between the FECA and the Internal Revenue Code, a gap largely created by the gray area of "issue advocacy," provided political groups with a loophole that they rapidly began to exploit in anticipation of the 2000 election. Specifically, groups began to form under Section 527 for the express purpose of raising and spending unlimited sums on issue advocacy. This tactic allowed them to avoid federal campaign finance regulations and federal taxation, thus providing them with a secret and unrestricted ability to participate in election campaigns.

In the first months of 2000, Common Cause identified a dozen such organizations. One of these entities, the Republican Majority Issues Committee, which was associated with House Majority Whip Tom DeLay (R-Texas), planned to spend $25 million on voter mobilization efforts and issue advertising to promote the election of Republicans in key House races. Another group, Citizens for the Republican Congress, which was formed by former representative Pat Saiki (R-Hawaii) and a group of Republican lawyers and consultants, reportedly hoped to raise $35 million for advertisements to be aired in the thirty most competitive House races. Similarly, the Sierra Club formed a Section 527 committee to broadcast advertisements against George W. Bush during the presidential primaries and to engage in issue advocacy in more than twenty congressional races during the general election.[25]

These committees and others raised the prospect of widespread circumvention of federal campaign finance laws. In an uncharacteristic move given the history of campaign finance reform, Congress swiftly reacted to this development and passed legislation that places disclosure requirements on certain Section 527 organizations.[26] This law, the first major change in federal campaign finance rules since 1979, imposed reporting obligations on Section 527 political organizations that have annual gross receipts in excess of $25,000 and are not required to report with the FEC. All Section 527 organizations that meet the revenue threshold must file annual income tax returns similar to Form 990 filed with the IRS by unions and other organizations that are tax exempt under Section 501 of the tax code. In addition, these organizations must report all contributors of $200 or more during a calendar year and expenditures of more than $500 to any one source in a calendar year.

Congress thus placed a minimal reporting requirement on these organizations. It did not impose any limits on funding or prohibit any issue advocacy activities. How it will work in practice is uncertain, but what is certain is that this latest reform does not obviate the pressing need for broad reform of the campaign finance system.

8

OPTIONS FOR REFORM

The failures of the FECA, and the financial innovations that have emerged in response to the law, have convinced most Americans of the need to change the campaign finance system. But the nature of any change has become a matter of substantial public debate. While many solutions have been offered, none of them addresses all of the problems revealed in recent elections or satisfies all of the objectives advocates hope to achieve in regulating political finance. Activists therefore remain divided as to the best approach to reform. Consequently, few alternatives have gained broad political support, and even those that have achieved this support have faced significant political opposition.

Politicians on both sides of the aisle and policy experts representing diverse perspectives have advanced a wide array of campaign finance reforms. This broad range of solutions is reflected in the bills submitted in recent sessions of Congress. More than 130 bills to amend the FECA were introduced in the 105th Congress (1997–98), and at least 50 were submitted in the 106th Congress (1999–2000). These proposals cover the full spectrum of possible approaches, extending from the repeal of the FECA and a return to a privately funded, deregulated system to the elimination of private contributions to candidates and full public funding of campaigns.

Despite this panoply of alternatives, the legislative debate since 1996 has centered on reforms designed to address the issues raised by soft money and

95

issue advocacy, along with a major Republican proposal to limit regulation and emphasize public disclosure. This represents a major change from previous Congresses, when the emphasis was on additional restrictions for PAC financing, some form of voluntary public subsidies for congressional campaigns (usually in the form of free or reduced-cost broadcast time for candidates or subsidized mailings), and spending limits on congressional campaigns. With the growth of soft money and issue advocacy spending, PAC contributions and expenditures came to be seen as one of the more legitimate forms of campaign finance, and therefore less of a reform priority because these contributions were limited by the FECA and subject to full disclosure. In comparison, soft money financing was wholly unlimited and issue advocacy spending subject to no regulation at all. Moreover, the failure of numerous attempts between 1986 and 1996 to pass a bill that sought to reduce PAC funding or to establish public subsidies and spending limits gave credence to the view that reformers would have better luck by simply trying to address the most grievous abuses.[1] This position was also more pragmatic, given the election of a Republican majority in 1994, which was unlikely to support any proposal that included public subsidies and spending limits.

The legislative debate has been framed by three broad issues. First, what changes can be made that will not violate First Amendment principles and thus will withstand a challenge in the courts? Legislators do not want to repeat the experience with the FECA in which Congress adopts a system of regulation only to have major portions of the law struck down by the courts for violating the right to free speech. This concern is particularly relevant given that the central provisions of most of the major proposals would impose greater restrictions on the types of financial activity than some courts have recently deemed to be protected under the First Amendment.

Second, what changes will best protect the political system from corruption or other undue influence that can accompany political contributions? Soft money and issue advocacy have resurrected the concerns about the corruptive influence of large contributions that originally led to the passage of the FECA. Most advocates of reform therefore have argued that no legislative package will be meaningful unless it addresses the problem of large contributions.

Third, what changes can be made that will not encourage new or unforeseen consequences that will undermine the effectiveness of any new law? Many legislators have concluded that the FECA's regulatory structure encouraged candidates and other political participants to seek out loopholes in the law and pursue innovative practices that undermined the efficacy of federal regulation. Any future reform therefore must include provisions that anticipate loopholes and guard against circumvention of the law.

There are no simple answers to these questions. Public officials and policy specialists reach different conclusions depending on their ideological perspectives, partisan considerations, political opinions, and judgments concerning the importance of various objectives associated with campaign finance law. The complexity of the issues also complicates the debate, with policy preferences often dependent on one's prediction of the relative effects of different legal provisions. These factors explain the variety of approaches and reforms that have been proposed in recent years.[2] They also explain why Congress has had difficulty resolving the competing arguments advanced in the debate and agreeing on a comprehensive bill that would fix the current system.

DEREGULATION AND DISCLOSURE

The failure of the FECA has led some policymakers to conclude that any system designed to control campaign contributions and expenditures will be ineffective. Stringent regulation will simply encourage candidates and other participants to seek out new ways to get around the rules, just as they have done under the FECA. So instead of engaging in what is likely to be a futile effort to regulate campaign funding further, these policymakers believe Congress should adopt a more practical and enforceable approach. This approach would eliminate many of the restrictions of the FECA and move to a regulatory framework that simply provides for full public disclosure of campaign finances.

Deregulation is the idea behind the "Doolittle bill," which emerged as a major Republican alternative for FECA reform in the 105th Congress. This proposal, sponsored by Representative John Doolittle (R-California), calls for expedited and expanded disclosure, the elimination of all federal contribution limits, and the termination of the public funding program.[3] The bill is based on the notion that political contributions and expenditures constitute political speech and that the purpose of campaign finance laws should be to promote political speech and provide the electorate with the information needed to make informed decisions. It therefore eliminates all federal campaign contribution limits and terminates the federal tax checkoff program and taxpayer financing of elections. It modifies current disclosure and reporting requirements by "requiring mandatory electronic filing" of disclosure reports, as opposed to the current law, which "permits" electronic filing. It also extends current disclosure rules by requiring any state or local party committee that has to file a report of its disbursements under state or local law also to file a copy of the report with the FEC. The effect of this latter provision would be to require state and local committees to report all expenditures to the FEC, which would make it easier to determine how state and local party committees are spending funds, including soft monies transferred to them from national party committee coffers.

The Doolittle bill offers the least restrictive and simplest model of reform. Instead of a complex web of rules and restrictions, the law would allow candidates to conduct campaigns as they desire, with all financial transactions reported to the public. The federal system thus would be comparable to the system used in state and local elections in Virginia and other states without contribution limits, where it has proved to be an effective approach for the funding of campaigns.[4] It would be the easiest law to administer and enforce because it requires candidates and party committees only to file disclosure reports. There are no other restrictions. Candidates may raise and spend as much as they can, and donors may give or spend as much as they choose without any limit on contributions. Supporters of this approach contend that such a system will enhance legal compliance since the elimination of contribution and spending ceilings will remove any incentive to circumvent the law and diminish the possibility of unexpected innovations in the years ahead.

Of all the alternatives, simple disclosure places the greatest value on free speech and considers the promotion of robust political debate as the main objective of campaign finance regulation. It moves beyond the Supreme Court's ruling in *Buckley* in holding that both expenditures and contributions are forms of political speech that should not be limited under the law. This approach will thus fulfill the central purpose of the First Amendment.

Another benefit advanced by adherents is that simple disclosure will improve the level of competition in federal elections. By eliminating contribution limits, this approach will make it easier for candidates to raise the funds needed to mount a campaign because they will no longer need to raise a relatively large number of contributions from a broad base of donors. Instead, a contender can rely on large gifts from a core of supporters to launch a campaign, as some candidates, such as 1968 presidential aspirants Eugene McCarthy and Robert Kennedy, did prior to the adoption of the FECA. It thus provides candidates with a better means of competing against wealthy rivals since it enhances the capacity of individuals to raise the funds needed to run against a self-financed opponent. Moreover, deregulation will help ensure that the candidates, especially incumbents, do not control the agenda in election campaigns or dominate the public debate since other participants will be able to raise funds and share their views about the candidates or the issues in an election without encountering federal restrictions.

This argument, however, assumes that challengers will be successful in raising the monies they need to compete effectively against incumbents, who will also be able to solicit unlimited contributions from donors. Given the financial patterns that have characterized federal elections for at least the past twenty-five years, it is likely that incumbents will maintain their already sizable fundraising advantage under an unregulated system. An unregulated regime is therefore unlikely to enhance the competitiveness of elections to the extent that some advocates claim. This is particularly so given that the effect of such a system will be to elevate significantly the levels of campaign fundraising and spending, thus raising the threshold amount considered necessary to wage a competitive campaign. Only those challengers with access to well-heeled donors are likely to be more viable than the challengers running under the present system.

Oppolnents of the disclosure model note that any increase in political speech or competition that might occur under such a system must be weighed against the increased threat of corruption or appearance of corruption that will accompany the abolition of restrictions. Deregulation promises the return of large contributions to candidates, thereby allowing candidates to solicit for their own campaigns the type of contributions now received by the national party committees in the form of soft money. Opponents argue that this will revive the role and influence of large donors in the political process and lead to the types of corruptive behavior and the appearance of undue influence that have long been a concern in American politics. They thus cast this approach as "deform" rather than "reform."

The Doolittle bill and similar reform proposals contend that disclosure provides a solution to the problem of corruption since it makes available to the public the information needed to assess potential undue influence. Electronic reporting will make all information from financial reports readily accessible and expose all transactions to public scrutiny. Citizens can then make judgments about the influence of donors on candidates or political committees. The system will thus provide a safeguard against corruption while enhancing political speech.

The problem with this defense is threefold. First, the Doolittle proposal provides only for limited disclosure. Basically, the plan calls for the disclosure of information that is already disclosed to the FEC, with no significant additions. It therefore fails to address the disclosure issues that have been raised in the recent campaign finance debates. The one change included in the Doolittle plan would be the compulsory filing of state party committee reports at the FEC (state party committees already are required to file reports on some of their financial activities with the FEC), but even in this instance the bill calls for the reporting only of disbursements, not of contributions, so that the monies raised by state party committees still would not be disclosed federally. It thus would be difficult to determine whether donors making contributions to the national committees also were giving to the state committees or whether donors were attempting to avoid disclosure by giving at the state level rather than the national level. Second, the plan does not include any provision for the disclosure of issue advocacy financing. Nor is it clear whether its provisions would extend to the type of party-building activities financed with soft money that are not considered to be express advocacy yet are now disclosed under FEC regulations. It therefore fails to address one of the central issues raised by advocates of greater regulation—the evasion of federal disclosure laws and the need to report issue advocacy spending.

This last concern raises the third problem with respect to the efficacy of a simple disclosure approach in addressing potential corruption: there is no guarantee of full compliance. While there will be less incentive on the part of most participants to evade the law, it is not necessarily the case that campaign donors or other financial participants will be more willing to adhere to the law under the Doolittle plan. Indeed, one of the factors behind the growth of issue advocacy spending and the corresponding opposition to issue advocacy regulation is the desire by some participants to keep their sources of financial support and political spending out of the public limelight. Disclosure alone will not address this problem unless it extends to other areas of political finance. Accordingly, most advocates of campaign finance reform have concluded that disclosure alone is not enough. Further changes are needed if a practicable and meaningful reform of the process is to be achieved.

REFORMING SOFT MONEY

Most campaign finance reforms submitted in recent Congresses call for more regulation, not less. These proposals seek to close the major "loopholes" in the FECA's regulatory structure by placing additional constraints on political funding and limiting the role of unregulated monies in the electoral process. The primary objective of these reforms is to resolve the issues associated with soft money.

The majority of participants in the campaign finance debate believe that no reform will be meaningful unless it puts an end to soft money contributions. While some experts and legislators, especially conservatives and strict interpreters of the First Amendment, contend that Congress lacks authority to limit soft money because it is not "campaign spending" or "express advocacy,"[5] most lawmakers and advocates believe that Congress has the power to impose limits on party fundraising and thus to address the soft money issue. Generally, those who support a ban on soft money or some other restriction consider regulation justified because it is necessary to prevent corruption or the appearance of corruption.

Legislators and policy experts alike differ as to the best approach for addressing this problem. The approach with the greatest political support in

Congress is the McCain-Feingold proposal (or its House counterpart, the Shays-Meehan bill), which calls for a complete ban on soft money financing.[6] This legislation has received the support of a majority in the House and Senate in each of the past two Congresses. In both instances, however, the proposal was blocked by a Senate filibuster mounted by Republican Mitch McConnell of Kentucky. Consequently, the debate over soft money continues, with alternative proposals now being advanced that are designed either to attract greater Republican support or to have less of an effect on party funding than a total ban on soft money.

The differences over soft money reform are generally due to differing views on the role of party funding and the scope of federal authority to restrict the financial activities of state and local parties. Some proposals want to mitigate the effect of soft money reform on party finances and thus call for caps on soft money contributions or increases in hard money limits to provide some compensation for the reduction in soft money. The major proposals also differ on the extent of federal regulation, with one approach banning soft money at the national level and another extending this prohibition to certain aspects of state and local party funding.

Those who support the role of parties in the political process or are concerned about the health of the national party organizations note that party funding can play a valuable role in the political process.[7] Parties are a major source of financial support for federal candidates. This is especially true for challengers and open-seat candidates, who are the primary recipients of party contributions and coordinated expenditures. Party spending on voter contact programs, voter mobilization, and other election-related activities helps to promote citizen participation, to relieve candidates of the need to finance such activities on their own, and to eliminate much of the overlap that can occur when individual contenders under the same party banner are each trying to encourage party supporters to vote. Some observers also note that adequate party financing is essential for limiting the potential influence of issue advocacy advertising or for responding to independent expenditures by organized groups. A candidate who faces such expenditures may not have the resources needed to respond to these communications, especially if they occur in the final week of an election campaign. A party committee can therefore play an important role by responding on the candidate's behalf.

These considerations have led some advocates of soft money reform to call for some combination of soft money limits, increased contribution limits, or changes in party committee hard money rules to provide some compensation for the revenue that would be lost (more than $200 million in each of the past two election cycles) as a result of a limit or total ban on party soft money.[8]

THE HAGEL PLAN

Senator Chuck Hagel (R-Nebraska) has introduced legislation that would place a cap on party soft money contributions.[9] Under his plan, soft money contributions to a national party committee, a congressional campaign committee, or some other committee under a national committee's maintenance or control would be limited to a total of $60,000 per calendar year, with the amount adjusted for inflation each calendar year. The solicitation of these contributions would be prohibited in federal buildings. Otherwise, there are no restrictions on the solicitation of soft money gifts. The bill also triples all hard money contribution limits to account roughly for inflation since the limits were established. If adopted, a candidate could receive an individual contribution of up to $3,000 per election, a PAC contribution of up to $15,000 per election, and the aggregate individual limit would be increased to $75,000. An individual could contribute $60,000 in hard money to a national party committee, as opposed to the current limit of $20,000. The proposal would thus limit the amount an individual could give to a party in any one year to a maximum of $120,000 ($60,000 in hard money and $60,000 in soft money). All of these ceilings would be adjusted annually to account for inflation.

THE BUSH PLAN

Governor George W. Bush of Texas, the 2000 Republican nominee for president, proposed another approach to soft money reform in a campaign finance reform plan he announced on February 15, 2000.[10] This plan takes a more restrictive approach to the regulation of soft money than that offered by Hagel or most other Republican congressional leaders. The basic principle informing the proposal is that elections should be financed through the voluntary contributions made by individuals and that other sources of funding should be prohibited in federal elections. The Bush plan thus would impose a partial ban on soft money contributions by prohibiting contributions by corporations and labor unions. Individuals, however, would still be allowed to make unlimited soft money gifts. In addition, the Bush plan would increase the limit on hard money contributions made to candidates by individuals.

The Bush proposal addresses the major objection raised against the Hagel plan, which is the argument that Hagel's approach would have relatively little effect in reducing the influence of large contributions in the political system since soft money donors could give up to $60,000 a year and individuals could give up to $120,000 per year to a party ($60,000 in hard money in addition to $60,000 in soft money). By prohibiting corporate and labor contributions to national party committees, the Bush plan would significantly reduce the amount of soft money at the national level. If current patterns are taken as a baseline, more than half of the soft money now raised would be eliminated under this plan.

The major problem with the proposal, which is also a flaw in the Hagel plan in the minds of many reformers, is that it would only apply to national party committees and would not prevent corporations or labor unions, as well as individuals, from making soft money gifts to state party committees. Consequently, the partial ban imposed on national committees could be easily circumvented by directing funds to state party coffers. Opponents of the proposal consider such evasion likely, particularly because the Bush plan calls for no additional rules to restrict the use of soft money by party committees, especially its use to finance issue advertising. As a result, there will remain a high demand for soft money dollars, which will provide a strong incentive to party organizations to circumvent the law. This concern has led many policymakers, including a group of House freshmen in recent Congresses, to call for a more extensive approach to soft money reform.

THE "FRESHMAN BILL"

As noted earlier, working from a somewhat similar but more restrictive line of thinking, a bipartisan group of House freshmen in the 105th Congress introduced a reform plan, which came to be known as the "Freshman bill," that would have prohibited soft money contributions, while increasing the opportunities for parties to raise and spend hard money.[11] The bill essentially adopted a provision of the McCain-Feingold legislation in stating that national party committees would be prohibited from soliciting, receiving, directing, transferring, or spending soft money. In addition, the bill would prohibit federal candidates or officials from raising soft money for federal elections, raising monies from sources beyond federal restriction in nonfederal elections, or raising soft money for advertising messages that refer to federal candidates (for example, issue ads featuring specific federal candidates). The only funds federal candidates could raise that were not subject to federal limits would be those they might raise for their own races for nonfederal office (for example, a U.S. representative raising money for her own race for governor in a state with higher contribution limits than those established by federal law). Federal candidates also would be allowed to attend state party fundraisers in their home states. Finally, the bill would ban transfers between state parties of soft money, meaning funds not permitted at the federal level. So party organizations could not try to circumvent the federal restriction by transferring large sums of soft money from state to state (as opposed to the transfers from the national committees to the states that take place under the present system).

In exchange for this ban on soft money, the Freshman approach increases the capacity of the national committees to raise hard money and increases their freedom to spend it on behalf of candidates. Under the FECA, individuals may contribute no more than $20,000 per year to a national party committee, with that amount subject to the aggregate individual limit of $25,000 for all contributions made by an individual to federal candidates, PACs, and party committees. The Freshman bill calls for an increase in the hard money limit for individual party contributions to $25,000 per year. It also provides for a change in the annual aggregate limit so that there would be two separate aggregate limits for individuals: a limit of $25,000 per year for all contributions to candidates and PACs and a separate annual aggregate limit of $25,000 for all contributions to party committees.

Furthermore, the Freshman bill would significantly expand the ability of parties to spend money on behalf of their candidates. The plan repeals the ceilings on coordinated expenditures, creating the opportunity for parties to spend unlimited amounts in support of a contender who is opposed by a wealthy, self-financed candidate or to respond to independent expenditures or issue advocacy expenditures made against a party contender by outside groups.

A major advantage of the Freshman approach and similar reform proposals is that they seek to balance the concerns about corruption that accompany large contributions with the legitimate interests of the party organizations and the benefits parties provide in the form of improved competition and voter choice. Another strength is that this approach would be more likely to endure a court challenge since it is focused on eliminating the potentially corruptive influence of unregulated soft money gifts while at the same time acknowledging the role of party organizations in the electoral process and expanding their ability to engage in political activity along the lines of the principles set forth in the *Colorado* decision.

Despite these advantages, this effort to reform soft money is criticized from both sides of the political aisle. Some Republicans and First Amendment scholars argue that since party soft money financing is not used for express advocacy, and because the corruptive influence of soft money contributions has not been clearly documented, a ban on soft money will not withstand constitutional scrutiny. Others, including party advocates, claim that the approach will significantly reduce the role of parties in the political process since the hard money adjustments will not wholly compensate for the loss of soft money revenues. This undoubtedly will be true, especially under the Freshman bill. Most of the soft money comes from corporations, which will be banned from giving under its provisions, and the largest individual donors will have to reduce the amounts they give substantially (for example, the Freshman bill permits individuals to give up to $25,000 a year, a sum that is well below the amounts now donated by the larger soft money donors). Even so, the plan will leave the parties with revenues substantially greater than the total amounts they received less than ten years ago. For example, in 1988, the two major parties raised a total of about $424 million in hard and soft money; in 1998, they raised $431 million in hard money alone.

The more important arguments advanced against this more incremental approach toward soft money reform come from public citizen groups such as Common Cause, Public Citizen, and Public Campaign, as well as many of the lawmakers who support McCain-Feingold. These critics contend that the Freshman model is inadequate for two major reasons. First, such a plan does not provide an adequate safeguard against corruption or the undue influence of a relatively small group of wealthy donors. In their view, the increase in contribution limits is too high to ensure the integrity of the political process and the promotion of political equality, which they regard as primary objectives of any regulatory scheme. These goals are not fostered by rules that allow individuals to contribute $25,000 or $50,000 or more to the national party committees. At this level, they observe, the donors would constitute an elite who would enjoy greater access and influence than the more than nine out of ten members of the electorate who contribute no money at all in federal elections.[12]

Second, opponents of the more moderate approach in the Freshman bill note that it will be easily circumvented. Advocates of a total ban on soft money contend that a ban that extends only to the national party committees simply will encourage soft money to flow directly to the states, where it will be even more difficult to trace than under the current system. State party chairs and state elected officials will raise soft money funds from established party donors without relying on any efforts by federal candidates or elected officials or national party staff, and then they will spend these funds on activities designed to benefit federal candidates.

THE MCCAIN-FEINGOLD PROPOSAL

These two basic criticisms of incremental approaches are a large part of the reason why the majority in Congress has come to support the McCain-Feingold bill, which advocates a much more stringent regulatory approach. As with the Freshman bill, it calls for a ban on soft money at the national level. But the McCain-Feingold legislation (or Shays-Meehan, which follows the same approach) goes a step further. It bans state or local party soft money financing for any federal election activity, defined as registration drives that occur in the last 120 days of a federal election, voter identification and get-out-the-vote drives, messages referring to federal candidates with an intent to influence elections (candidate-specific issue ads), or other generic party activities where a federal candidate is on the ballot. In short, election-related activities that might influence the outcome of a federal election, even if conducted by a state or local party, must be financed with funds subject to federal contribution limits. Soft money can be used only on strictly nonfederal activities.

This "state-level" prohibition on soft money funding in connection with federal elections certainly enhances the potential effectiveness of a soft money ban. It is more restrictive than the state-to-state transfer prohibition included in the Freshman bill because it brings some types of soft money expenditures under federal restrictions, which is not the case under the Freshman bill. But this strength is also its major weakness since it exposes the reform to a much greater likelihood of succumbing to a constitutional challenge. While the provision makes the law more effective, it limits contributions and spending on activities that may "influence" federal elections or are "election-related." To date, the majority of court opinions, beginning with the Supreme Court's ruling in Buckley, have held that such language is too vague and overbroad to withstand constitutional scrutiny. The courts have therefore, in most instances, struck down regulations that seek to restrict campaign funding that may "influence" election outcomes or simply entail "election-related speech" rather than express advocacy. In addition, because this type of activity does not constitute "express advocacy," it is a particularly open question as to whether such a regulation would withstand judicial review.

Another argument advanced against McCain-Feingold is that it will place too great a burden on the party organizations and thus reduce their role in the electoral process. Recent versions of McCain-Feingold provide for only a $5,000 increase in the amount that an individual may contribute to the parties, much less than the increases provided by the Freshman bill or Hagel plan. The legislation also retains party-coordinated spending limits (the Freshman bill would abolish them) and further restricts such spending by banning parties from making coordinated expenditures on behalf of a general election candidate who spends more than $50,000 in personal funds on the campaign. The plan also would change the definition of what constitutes coordination or cooperation between a political committee and candidate, and it would prohibit a party committee from making both coordinated and independent expenditures in connection with the election of a single candidate. Those who support an expanded role for parties thus view the McCain-Feingold plan less favorably than other alternatives.

REFORMING ISSUE ADVOCACY

Even greater constitutional controversy surrounds proposals to regulate issue advocacy advertising. Some observers regard issue advocacy as a fundamental example of protected political speech that is essential to the creation of a more informed electorate. Others consider it the ultimate subterfuge that has allowed well-funded interests wholly to evade the FECA's regulatory regime. And then there are those in between, who are struggling to find a workable compromise on this particularly difficult issue.

One approach to issue advocacy advertising is to make no change in the current regulatory framework and allow this type of political expression to continue to operate beyond the scope of campaign finance law. This is the preferred position of many First Amendment scholars and enjoys the greatest support in the courts. Put simply, the argument here is that the law should conform to the "magic words" doctrine established by the courts as a bright line to distinguish political speech that Congress may regulate from speech that it cannot. One advantage of this approach is that it gives the broadest protection to free speech.

Most advocates of reform, however, are unwilling to abide by the status quo. As the elections of 1996 and 1998 have clearly demonstrated, unless this activity is brought within the scope of federal regulation, it will stand as a vehicle that can be exploited by individuals, party committees, and organized groups to raise and spend unlimited amounts of money from unlimited and undisclosed sources in ways that are clearly designed to influence the election of specific candidates.

Legislators and policy experts who support changes such as those contained in the Freshman bill or McCain-Feingold have increasingly concluded that soft money reform will be ineffective unless something is done about issue advocacy. Their fear is that tightening the rules on soft money, absent issue advocacy reform, will simply cause donors to shift their giving to issue advocacy groups. It will encourage money to move out of the soft money arena, which is at least subject to FECA disclosure rules, into the issue advocacy realm, which is not subject to any FECA regulation. The opponents of further regulation raise the counterargument, however, that all of this means more speech and that the links to corruption remain to be demonstrated.

Both McCain-Feingold and Shays-Meehan have taken a strong stand on the question of issue advocacy and set forth the broadest change currently under consideration in the reform debate. Their idea is to broaden the definition of express advocacy to include certain types of issue advocacy advertising, specifically those communications that advocates of reform, such as Common Cause, usually cast as "sham issue ads." This approach would expand the "magic words" test to include other standards for determining whether a communication meets the express advocacy test. Specifically, it would include any broadcast, newspaper, magazine, billboard, direct mail, or similar type of public communication that: (1) refers to a clearly identified federal candidate; (2) would be understood by a reasonable person as advocating the election or defeat of the candidate; and (3) is made within thirty days before a primary (and is targeted at the state in which the primary is occurring) or sixty days before a general election.

Communications that met these criteria would be subject to federal campaign finance restrictions. This proposal would thus require disclosure of the amounts raised and spent on the ads that met the new legal definitions. It also would require that these ads be paid for from monies subject to federal campaign finance limitations. In other words, groups or organizations that wanted to engage in such communications could continue to do so, but they would have to pay for them with hard money. This proposal would essentially treat candidate-specific issue ads broadcast or otherwise distributed in proximity to an election in a manner comparable to independent expenditures under current law.

The major problem with this approach is that it is the least likely to withstand a court challenge. While not exactly following the test upheld by the court in the *Furgatch* decision, it is based on the rationale of *Furgatch* and attempts to establish a more narrowly defined test for regulation than the standard suggested in *Furgatch*. The FEC has already promulgated regulations that attempted to implement a *Furgatch*-based standard and to expand the concept of express advocacy, but these rules were struck down in district court because they violated the "magic words" standard.[13]

Opponents also note that an expanded conception of express advocacy might have a chilling effect on political speech. They contend that the regulatory burden imposed on groups or individuals to register a committee with the FEC and disclose finances may discourage this type of speech. They further claim that it might discourage individuals from contributing to groups that engage in issue advocacy because they do not want their donor information publicly disclosed. This also raises a constitutional question concerning the right to anonymous speech. While the Supreme Court upheld required disclosure in *Buckley* as a means of deterring corruption and encouraging a more informed electorate, the Court has issued other rulings in which it has supported speakers' claims to anonymous speech, even when those claims for anonymity were made in a political debate context and deemed to undermine the objective of a more informed electorate.[14]

Finally, critics of the McCain-Feingold plan note that the reform might simply encourage groups and organizations to spend more money on issue advocacy in the period before the pre-election time periods that trigger stricter regulation. Advocates, however, contend that such spending would be less effective than advertising done in the weeks leading up to an election.

As to the constitutional arguments, supporters of McCain-Feingold believe that their proposal is tailored narrowly enough and establishes a standard that is clear enough to withstand judicial scrutiny. Others who desire reform are not so certain, and thus have advanced alternative solutions. The bipartisan Freshman bill sought to resolve this problem by moving more slowly on the regulation of issue advocacy. In the proponents' view, a narrowly tailored disclosure approach offered the best hope of passing constitutional muster and a better prospect of attracting Republican support. They therefore advanced a reform proposal that would require disclosure of issue advocacy spending when certain expenditure thresholds on broadcast communications were reached.

Under this proposal, persons or organizations that broadcast communications that mention or include (by name, representation, or likeness) a specific candidate for federal office would have to disclose the amount of their expenditure. But in order to ensure that disclosure does not impose too great a burden on political speakers, this requirement would apply only to communications that reach certain spending thresholds. Any person or organization that expends more than $25,000 in a calendar year on broadcast communications mentioning a federal candidate is subject to disclosure requirements. In order to discourage efforts to circumvent this rule, any individual or organization that spends an aggregate of $100,000 per calendar year on such communications also must disclose spending. Disclosure is required within seven days of reaching the threshold amount, and within twenty-four hours if this occurs during the last ten days of an election.

Since disclosure is tied to certain candidate-specific messages, sets expenditure thresholds, and is focused on broadcast expenditures, it is much more likely to survive judicial scrutiny than the McCain-Feingold plan.[15] For example, it is much less likely to require disclosure by small groups or individuals spending relatively small sums on their own; it is therefore less likely to be perceived as an unnecessary or undue burden on political speech. The problem, of course, is that the disclosure requirement does not extend far enough; it does not include the sources of funding and the amounts of contributions.

One of the central purposes of disclosure, a purpose recognized by the courts, is that it allows the public to know who is attempting to influence their votes and how much is being spent to do so. Disclosure of receipts and expenditures will thus increase the level of accountability. So long as the disclosure requirement is narrowly tailored and allows individuals the option of demonstrating to regulators or the courts that they are justified in remaining anonymous due to fear of reprisal, harassment, or one of the other exemptions the courts have traditionally recognized, it is likely that the courts would uphold it.[16] But this, too, is a constitutional question that will probably not be resolved until it is tested in court.

PROVIDING "PAYCHECK PROTECTION"

The concerns about the efficacy of soft money regulations and the constitutionality of proposed issue advocacy regulations have led some elected officials and advocates of reform to search for ways in which to alter the sources
of soft money and issue advocacy contributions rather than the spending of the
money. Others, primarily Republicans, have sought to extend restrictions to
encompass other activities beyond those conducted by the party committees
but only for a particular type of organization, labor unions. Espousing the principle that any monies used for political activities should be voluntarily donated, these lawmakers contend that no "involuntary contributions" should be
permitted in federal political activity. Specifically, union dues should be used
only for political efforts if a member has agreed to this use.

The basic thrust of the proposal, which has come to be known as "paycheck protection" and is included among the central provisions of George
Bush's reform plan, is to eliminate the use of labor union treasury funds for
political activity unless the monies come from voluntary contributions, not
mandatory dues, fees, or other payments required as a condition of employment. (PAC monies are already voluntary under the law; all monies raised
and spent by labor PACs must come from voluntary contributions that are
limited by law.)

The principle is drawn from the Supreme Court's decision in *Communications
Workers of America* v. *Beck*.[17] In the *Beck* decision, the Supreme Court determined that the National Labor Relations Act limited union use of money
raised from nonunion employees as a condition of employment to support col-
lective bargaining (known as "agency agreements"). As a result, nonunion
employees in closed shops cannot be required to fund political spending as a
condition of their employment. Accordingly, the National Labor Relations
Board in *California Saw & Knife Works*[18] established rules that allow nonunion
members under agency agreements to object to paying for activities "not ger-
mane to the union's duties as a bargaining agent" and allow them to receive a
reduction in fees representing the share of payments that are devoted to the
objectionable activities.

As might be expected, this proposal is adamantly opposed by labor unions
and many Democratic officeholders since the vast majority of labor expenditures have benefited Democrats. The reform has a distinctly partisan cast
(most versions contain no comparable provision for corporate treasury funds)
and is considered a "poison pill" by Democrats—designed to kill any reform bill
that gets to a vote. Union leaders further contend that such a provision inter-
feres with their right to represent their membership. They also note that corporate shareholders do not have the right to vote on whether to approve

corporate political spending. They therefore demand that any regulations concerning voluntary contributions applied to labor unions be equitably imposed on corporations in order to ensure some measure of fairness.

This issue has become noteworthy in the legislative deadlock over campaign finance reform. In an effort to provide an alternative, some legislators have proposed extending the principle of voluntary contributions to tax-exempt organizations and corporations, as well as labor unions. One amendment to McCain-Feingold proposed in the 105th Congress[19] would require that any monies spent by banks and corporations for "political activities" must come from voluntary contributions. The amendment would require banks and corporations to provide notice of any political expenditures to shareholders and any individuals who pay dues, initiation fees, or other payments and give them the right to decide whether funds should be allocated to this use. The notice would include (1) an estimate of the budget for political activities for not more than the next year, (2) a detailed itemization of all amounts disbursed for political activities in the preceding two years, and (3) an estimate of the dollar amount of each individual's dues, fees, or payments that will be used for political activities for not more than the next year.

What effect these proposals would have on labor and corporate political activity is difficult to discern since this subject has not been a focal point of congressional hearings or intensive analysis.

PUBLIC FUNDING

Soft money and issue advocacy reform do little to address the problems associated with the rising cost of campaigns or the emphasis placed on money in congressional elections. Nor do they, in most instances, address the issue of providing more resources to candidates so that they are better able to finance their campaigns.

One solution to these problems is to allow candidates to raise more money by permitting them to receive larger contributions. This is the alternative offered by advocates of the Doolittle approach and supporters of increased contribution limits. But this solution is anathema to those reformers who are already concerned about the role of private money in the electoral process and believe that candidates are now spending too much or that costs are too high. These reformers believe that campaign finance law should be designed to reduce the influence of private money and enhance the equity of citizen participation in the process. They therefore support more comprehensive and fundamental approaches to campaign finance reform that include some form of voluntary public subsidy or public financing, usually accompanied by campaign spending limits.

The basic idea behind public subsidies is to reduce the cost of campaigns so that a greater number of citizens can afford to run for office. In addition, public funding represents an alternative that should encounter no constitutional problems because the courts have already sanctioned the constitutionality of voluntary public subsidies and the imposition of spending limits as a condition of accepting this benefit.

In recent Congresses, however, there has been little support for a public financing scheme or public matching funds program for congressional candidates similar to the one used in presidential elections. Opponents cite the experience of the presidential public funding program and its spending limits as an example of the ineffectiveness of such an approach. They contend that public subsidies will amount to little more than "welfare for politicians," since such an approach will provide elected officials with a benefit that will have little effect on campaign spending or electoral competition because it will simply encourage evasions and circumventions of the law. Moreover, critics note that the public does not support such reforms, citing the rate of participation in the federal income tax checkoff as an indicator of public sentiment.

Despite this opposition, which primarily comes from Republican legislators and conservative activists, public funding has become an important component of the current debate. The principal legislative proposals, however, have not called for public financing. Instead, they have suggested some other form of subsidy in an effort to reduce opposition and minimize criticisms about the use of taxpayer dollars for campaign spending. Most bills therefore offer some sort of partial benefit that can supplement private fundraising activities, such as reduced rates for postage, reduced rates to purchase broadcast advertising, or free television time. These benefits would increase candidates' access to resources without entailing significant costs at the expense of taxpayers.

This partial subsidy approach was part of the original McCain-Feingold and Shays-Meehan proposals, which were submitted to Congress prior to 1996. These bills would have provided candidates with the option of receiving reduced-cost broadcasting time or reduced-cost mailings in exchange for the acceptance of campaign spending limits. Specifically, House candidates would receive these benefits if they agreed to: (1) limit their spending; (2) limit their use of personal funds; (3) raise a certain amount of their campaign monies in small contributions; and (4) raise a certain percentage of their campaign monies from in-state donors. Senate candidates would receive thirty minutes of free television time, as well as reduced-cost broadcast time and mailings, in exchange for: (1) accepting campaign spending limits; (2) agreeing to raise a certain share of their campaign monies from in-state donors; (3) agreeing to limit the use of personal funds; and (4) agreeing to raise a certain percentage of their campaign monies in the last two years of the six-year election cycle. In

1997, these provisions were separated from other parts of the McCain-Feingold and Shays-Meehan legislation in an effort to reduce Republican opposition to the legislation and improve the prospects for passing soft money and issue advocacy reform.[20] While the details differ from other free or reduced-cost broadcast time plans, the provisions are fairly representative of this approach to reform.

FREE TELEVISION TIME

The idea of offering candidates some amount of free television time is a particularly popular reform. The basic concept is that each broadcast licensee would set aside a certain amount of time each election cycle, usually about two hours, that would be made available to candidates. How this time would be allocated among the candidates is a difficult logistical issue, and most proposals would make the political parties responsible for these decisions. Some plans also call for regulations on how this time might be used, either by specifying the length of an ad (for example, no ads of less than a minute) or by requiring certain formats (for example, the candidate must appear in the ad). These provisions are based on the view that free time also could be used to improve the quality of political discourse in federal elections by encouraging ads longer than thirty seconds or requiring that candidates appear in the ads and directly address voters, instead of using the time to broadcast a negative campaign ad.

Some advocates of subsidies see them as a means of providing candidates with a floor of financial assistance. These observers consider subsidies to be a means of providing candidates, especially challengers, with the minimum level of resources needed to communicate their views to the electorate. Subsidies thus would help to improve competition in elections while also reducing the amount of funding needed to conduct a campaign.

Others, however, contend that subsidies without contingent spending limits will have little effect on rising campaign costs since candidates will take the public subsidy in whatever form it is offered and then go out and raise private funding just as they do under the present system. A majority of the bills that call for some form of subsidy therefore link this assistance to spending limits. Indeed, the primary reason why public subsidies are popular among some reform activists is that they allow the establishment of a system of voluntary spending limits.

While some reformers continue to support spending limits as a means of controlling spiraling campaign costs, especially if the soft money and issue advocacy "loopholes" are closed, many others claim that congressional spending limits will only encourage new innovations and subterfuges, recreating the experience under the presidential public funding system. It also will serve to reinforce the advantages enjoyed by wealthy, self-financed candidates because they will be able to outspend opponents who have agreed to limits by even larger margins than is the case under the current system. Critics further note that such a system of spending limits would be difficult and costly to administer since varying limits would have to be established to account for the great diversity found in the 50 states and the 435 congressional districts. Monitoring compliance with such a wide array of ceilings by such a large number of candidates (perhaps hundreds of publicly funded congressional aspirants as opposed to less than two dozen presidential hopefuls) would require a sizable increase in the resources of the FEC. Finally, any proposal for free time also faces strong political opposition from the broadcasters.

Another issue raised by the partial subsidy alternative is the limited amount of assistance that it would provide candidates. The majority share of House and Senate campaign budgets is not devoted to the purchase of broadcast time or mail. In fact, many House candidates do not use broadcast advertising in conducting their campaigns, so free or low-cost broadcast time or reduced-cost mailings, which are usually limited to a few mailings, would not have a significant effect on the cost of their campaigns. There still will be substantial amounts of private money being raised and spent within the system. Some advocates of public funding have therefore concluded that the best and most comprehensive approach to reform is to call for full public funding of elections.

CLEAN MONEY

Full public funding, which is sometimes called the "Clean Money" reform option, is an alternative that has not gathered much support in Congress but has received increasing attention in a handful of states.[21] Under this approach, which is championed by the public interest group Public Campaign and has been recognized by the American Civil Liberties Union as a constitutionally sanctioned alternative, candidates would be given the option to qualify for full public financing for their primary and general election campaigns. To be eligible for this subsidy, a candidate would simply have to raise a certain number of qualifying contributions from small donors and agree to forgo any additional funding and abide by campaign spending limits. If needed, a candidate would be allowed to raise a relatively small amount of "seed money" from private donors through small contributions to finance the solicitation of the qualifying contributions. Once qualified, a publicly funded candidate would have to conduct his or her campaign by relying solely on public money. The proposal seeks to reduce the disparity that might result in contests between publicly funded candidates and privately funded opponents by providing additional public monies to participating candidates who face opponents who privately spend more than allowed by the spending limit. In this way, the program provides additional public matching monies to allow candidates to equal the spending, up to a certain point, of nonpublicly funded opponents. This matching provision also applies to monies spent independently against a publicly funded candidate by a party committee or political group. In an effort to stem further the flow of private money in federal elections, supporters of the Clean Money option also support a ban on soft money and issue advocacy reform.

Federal legislators contend that such an approach does not present a viable alternative for reform since there is little legislative or public support for this option. Yet recent experience in some states suggests that this might not necessarily be the case. Since 1996, the states of Maine, Vermont, Massachusetts, and Arizona have adopted some version of the clean money option for use in elections for statewide officials and/or state legislative offices. In Maine, the first state to adopt the full public funding program for all statewide and state legislative campaigns, this reform has withstood a major legal challenge and is being used for the 2000 elections.[22] If the experiments now being conducted in the states provide empirical support for this bold approach to reform, it may gain greater prominence in the legislative debates in the years ahead.

THE GORE PROPOSAL

An interesting alternative that seeks to provide subsidies to candidates without moving to a full public funding model has recently been advanced by the Democratic presidential nominee, Vice President Al Gore. On March 27, 2000, Gore announced a campaign finance reform plan that included a ban on soft money (in the form of the McCain-Feingold approach), restrictions on issue advocacy (that include disclosure of the finances for ads broadcast within sixty days of an election), free broadcast time for candidates (five minutes each evening made available by broadcasters on each of the thirty nights before an election), and the creation of a "Democracy Endowment."[23]

The innovative aspect of the Gore plan is the Democracy Endowment, a public-private partnership managed by a board of trustees nominated by the president and approved by the Senate, which would finance the general election campaigns of qualified House and Senate candidates. The Endowment would be funded by contributions from individuals and corporations. Contributors would receive a 100 percent tax deduction for the amount of each contribution. This tax deduction provision would expire after seven years or when the Endowment achieves its financial goal, whichever threshold is reached first. The goal of the Endowment is to raise $7.1 billion in a seven-year period. This figure is based on estimates of the amount needed to meet the financial obligations of the campaign funding to be provided by the Endowment.

So instead of creating a system of public funding that is financed through a tax-checkoff system (as is the case in the current presidential public financing program) or legislative appropriations (as is the case in some state and local public financing programs), the Gore proposal promotes a hybrid system that is partly private, partly public. A public subsidy in the form of a 100 percent tax deduction is used to stimulate private contributions to the Endowment, which will then rely on interest earned from investments on the $7.1 billion to finance congressional campaigns. According to Gore, the total cost to the United States Treasury will be an estimated $2.13 billion over the course of the anticipated seven-year fundraising period, or an average annual cost of about $304 million.

Once the Endowment has been funded, monies will be made available to finance House and Senate general election campaigns. Candidates will qualify for funding by agreeing not to accept any other sources of funding and by agreeing to a campaign spending limit. The amount of the grant will equal the applicable general election campaign spending limit, which will be based on a combination of factors, including the average cost of previous House and Senate elections and, in the case of Senate races, the voting age population and media market characteristics of the state. Since the program is voluntary, candidates may choose not to participate and instead finance a campaign with private contributions or their own personal funds, as they do under the current campaign finance system. In order to discourage candidates from opting out of participation in the Endowment program, the trustees may supplement the amount of money given to a participating candidate to match the amount spent by a nonparticipating candidate or self-financed candidate.

If the fundraising for the Endowment falls short of the $7.1 billion goal by the end of the seven-year period in which the tax deduction is in place, then broadcasters—under the terms of the authorizing legislation—would be required to provide some amount of free television and radio time to candidates in order to make up for the shortfall.

This Endowment subsidy would not make any monies available to House and Senate candidates in primary elections. In the primaries, congressional candidates will continue to raise and spend funds as they do under the present system. The plan thus provides far less support for candidates than the full public funding option, or even the public matching funds approach used in the presidential system. Most important, it would provide no subsidies to challengers in primaries, which is the point in the election process when candidates seeking to compete against an incumbent are most in need of support. Further, the proposal places no constraints on donors to the Democracy Endowment with respect to additional political spending. Individual donors to the Endowment can continue to make contributions to candidates and political committees or continue to spend money independently in support of a candidate as is the case under the present system. This plan therefore is unlikely to attract significant support from those advocates of reform who believe that public funding is the most effective alternative. These reformers usually embrace public funding because it is a means of reducing or wholly replacing the role of private money in the system. The Gore proposal would not eliminate private funding. It is for this reason unlikely that supporters of such options as Clean Money reform would support this solution.

The success of this approach clearly depends on the ability to attract the private contributions needed to fund the Endowment. At an estimated $1 billion per year, the proposal calls for a level of funding that is essentially the equivalent of the total amount raised by all candidates, party committees, PACs, and independent spenders in federal elections in the 1996 election cycle. Whether a tax incentive will be a strong enough inducement, in combination with a desire to improve the campaign finance system, to encourage this level of giving is a legitimately debatable proposition. The efficacy of the tax incentive is particularly subject to question given the countervailing incentives against making such a contribution. These countervailing incentives include the fact that a contribution may be used to finance the campaign of a candidate that a donor would oppose, and the fact that the gift is not being given to a particular candidate or to a party committee for the support of a preferred candidate. If advocates of public funding are correct in assuming that private political contributions are primarily made to gain access or influence with particular politicians, then it is not likely that many of those who are now giving the large sums for political activity would be willing to contribute to the Endowment. The question may ultimately become that of whether the promise of the Endowment for improving the system, when combined with the tax incentive, will be enough to spur vast numbers of private citizens to give to this cause.

CONCLUSION

The rules governing political finance need to be reformed to account for the changes that have taken place in the years since the FECA was adopted. The majority of Americans consider this an essential first step toward improving the integrity of the electoral process and the quality of representation in government. How best to achieve these goals is a matter of great debate, and any solution is likely to involve a compromise and balancing of a variety of policy objectives and approaches to reform.

To date, Congress has not been able to develop a comprehensive alternative that can garner broad support from both sides of the political aisle or from different segments of the campaign finance reform policy community. There are many options available, and, as the recent proposals for deregulation, clean money, and even a national endowment suggest, the number of alternatives continues to expand as the dialogue continues. The best road to achieving a meaningful and effective reform of the process is to continue this dialogue and remain open to new evidence and proposals. For, as recent experience has shown, each election now brings with it new issues and new ideas that make it critical that some decision be reached on this thorny policy issue.

NOTES

CHAPTER 1

1. David E. Rosenbaum, "White House Guests Differ over Solicitation of Money," *New York Times*, September 17, 1997, p. A26; Tom Squitieri, "Campaign Fund-Raising Probe Turns Focus on Gore," *USA Today*, August 28, 1997, p. 7A; and Stephen Labaton, "Democrats Say They'll Return about $1.5 Million More in Questionable Gifts," *New York Times* (New England edition), March 1, 1997, p. 8.

2. Figure based on the expenditure data reported by the Federal Election Commission for presidential and congressional candidates, party organizations, political action committees, and other political organizations reporting expenditures in connection with federal elections. In 1992, the total amount spent in connection with federal elections was approximately $2.2 billion. For a breakdown of spending in 1992, see Herbert E. Alexander and Anthony Corrado, *Financing the 1992 Election* (Armonk, N.Y.: M. E. Sharpe, 1995), p. 5.

3. See Helen Dewar, "Campaign Reform's Uphill Fight," *Washington Post*, October 7, 1997, p. A5.

4. The McCain-Feingold bill was originally introduced as S. 25, while Shays-Meehan was introduced as H.R. 493. The Freshman proposal was introduced as H.R. 2183. For a discussion of the campaign finance debate in the 105th Congress, see Robert E. Mutch, "The Reinvigorated Reform Debate," in John C. Green, ed., *Financing the 1996 Election* (Armonk, N.Y.: M. E. Sharpe, 1999), chapter 9.

5. Alison Mitchell, "G.O.P., Relenting, Agrees to Take Up Campaign Finance," *New York Times*, April 23, 1998, p. A1.

6. Bob Hohler, "GOP to Curb Debate," *Boston Globe*, July 18, 1998, p. A3.

7. Bob Hohler, "Senate Foils Campaign Finance Bills," *Boston Globe*, October 20, 1999, p. A10.

CHAPTER 2

1. For a description of the major provisions of the 1971 FECA, see Anthony Corrado, "Federal Election Campaign Act of 1971," in L. Sandy Maisel, ed., *Political Parties and Elections in the United States: An Encyclopedia* (New York: Garland, 1991), I: 353–54.

2. 424 U.S. 1 (1976).

3. The original provisions of the 1974 FECA included a limit on the amount a candidate could spend out of personal funds or the funds of his or her immediate family, which was set at $50,000 for presidential candidates, $35,000 for Senate candidates, and $25,000 for House candidates; a limit of $1,000 on the amount spent independently by an individual or group; and varying limits on overall campaign spending in primary and general election campaigns for all candidates for federal office.

4. *Buckley* v. *Valeo*, 424 U.S. 40–45. See, in particular, note 52.

5. See, among others, *First National Bank of Boston* v. *Bellotti*, 435 U.S. 765 (1978); *Federal Election Commission* v. *Massachusetts Citizens for Life, Inc.*, 479 U.S. 238 (1986); *Austin* v. *Michigan State Chamber of Commerce*, 494 U.S. 652 (1990); *Federal Election Commission* v. *Christian Action Network*, 92 F.3d 1178 (4th Cir., 1996).

6. *Austin* v. *Michigan State Chamber of Commerce*, 494 U.S. 652 (1990).

7. 116 S.Ct. 2309 (1996).

8. Diana Dwyre, "Pushing the Campaign Finance Envelope: Parties and Interest Groups in the 1996 House and Senate Elections" (paper delivered at the Annual Meeting of the American Political Science Association, Washington, D.C., August 28–31, 1997), p. 35.

9. *Federal Election Commission* v. *Colorado Republican Federal Campaign Committee*, No. 89-N-1159 (D. Colo., February 18, 1999).

10. *Federal Election Commission* v. *Colorado Republican Federal Campaign Committee*, No. 99-1211 (10th Cir., May 5, 2000).

11. *Federal Election Commission* v. *Massachusetts Citizens for Life, Inc.*, 479 U.S. 238 (1986).

12. See 11 C.F.R. § 114.10. Under the law, "promotion of political ideas" is defined as issue advocacy, election-influencing activity, and research, training, or educational activity that is expressly tied to the organization's goals (11 C.F.R. § 114.10[b][1]).

13. There is an exception to this general rule: presidential general election campaigns can solicit contributions to pay for the legal and accounting costs incurred to comply with the law. All contributions received for these general election compliance funds are subject to federal contribution limits.

14. See 2 U.S.C. §431.

15. Federal Election Commission, Advisory Opinion 1978-10, August 29, 1978.

16. For a review of the court decisions on issue advocacy, see Trevor Potter, "Issue Advocacy and Express Advocacy," in Anthony Corrado et al., eds., *Campaign Finance Reform: A Sourcebook* (Washington, D.C.: Brookings Institution, 1997), pp. 227–39. Another approach to this issue is to look beyond the specific words in a message to determine if a communication presents an "electioneering message" that is clearly intended to encourage the audience to support or oppose a candidate. This was the approach adopted by the Ninth Circuit in deciding *Furgatch* v. *FEC* (807 F. 2d 857 [9th Cir., 1987]). Here the court ruled that speech without the "magic words" could amount to express advocacy if, when "read as a whole, and with limited reference to external events," a message is susceptible to no other reasonable interpretation than as "an exhortation to vote for or against a specific candidate" (at 864). The FEC has followed a similar approach in attempting to draft regulations to govern issue advocacy spending. But these regulations have already been successfully challenged in court in the First District, where the court decided that the proposed regulations were unconstitutional because they moved beyond the "magic words" test. See *Maine Right to Life Committee, Inc.* v. *FEC*, 914 F. Supp. 8 (D. Me., 1996).

CHAPTER 3

1. Herbert E. Alexander, "Spending in the 1996 Elections," in Green, *Financing the 1996 Election*, p. 17.

2. Alexander and Corrado, *Financing the 1992 Election*, p. 21.

3. Totals for congressional and presidential candidate spending based on data reported by the Federal Election Commission.

4. Based on data reported in Federal Election Commission, "FEC Reports on Congressional Fundraising for 1997–98," press release, April 28, 1999, pp. 1–2.

5. Joseph E. Cantor, *Congressional Campaign Spending: 1976–1996*, Congressional Research Service Report 97-793 GOV (Washington, D.C.: Library of Congress, August 1997), p. 1.

6. Alexander and Corrado, *Financing the 1992 Election*, p. 21; and Alexander, "Spending in the 1996 Elections," p. 17.

7. Major Garrett, *Money, Politics and the First Amendment*, Cato Institute Briefing Papers (Washington, D.C.: Cato Institute, June 19, 1997), p. 2.

8. Federal Election Commission, "FEC Reports on Congressional Fundraising for 1997–98," p. 1.

9. R. Craig Endicott, "Philip Morris Unseats P & G as Top Advertising Spender," *Advertising Age*, September 28, 1988, p. 1; and Alexander and Corrado, *Financing the 1992 Election*, p. 2.

10. Data reported in Joseph E. Cantor, Denis Steven Rutkus, and Kevin B. Greely, *Free and Reduced-Rate Television Time for Political Candidates* (Washington, D.C.:

Congressional Research Service, July 7, 1997), p. 5. It should be noted that the Television Bureau of Advertising estimates presented here represent only advertising purchased in the top seventy-five media markets, which cover 85 percent of the nation's television viewers.

11. Ira Chinoy, "In Presidential Race, TV Ads Were Biggest '96 Cost by Far," *Washington Post*, March 31, 1997, p. A19. These totals do not include the ads paid for by party committees on behalf of the presidential candidates.

12. Sarah Fritz and Dwight Morris, *Handbook of Campaign Spending: Money in the 1990 Congressional Races* (Washington, D.C.: Congressional Quarterly, 1992), pp. 53–54; Dwight Morris and Murielle E. Gamache, *Handbook of Campaign Spending: Money in the 1992 Congressional Races* (Washington, D.C.: Congressional Quarterly, 1994), pp. 6–10; and Dwight Morris and Murielle E. Gamache, *Gold-Plated Politics: The 1992 Congressional Races* (Washington, D.C.: Congressional Quarterly, 1994), p. 9.

13. Sarah Fritz and Dwight Morris, *Gold-Plated Politics: Running for Congress in the 1990s* (Washington, D.C.: Congressional Quarterly, 1992), pp. 14–26; and Morris and Gamache, *Gold-Plated Politics*, pp. 18–29.

14. Anthony Corrado, *Creative Campaigning* (Boulder, Colo.: Westview Press, 1992), p. 35; and Lee Ann Elliott, "Campaign Finance," *Journal of Law and Politics* 8 (Winter 1992): 302.

15. Spending totals based on figures reported by the Federal Election Commission.

16. Paul S. Herrnson, *Congressional Elections*, 2d ed. (Washington, D.C.: Congressional Quarterly, 1998), p. 48.

17. Craig Karmin, "Democrats Pin '96 Senate Hopes on Corporate Execs as Candidates," *The Hill*, November 22, 1995, p. 11.

18. Quoted in Garrett, *Money, Politics and the First Amendment*, p. 2.

19. Ibid., p. 3.

20. See Martin Schram, *Speaking Freely* (Washington, D.C.: Center for Responsive Politics, 1995), pp. 36–47.

CHAPTER 4

1. Larry Makinson, *The Big Picture: Money Follows Power Shift on Capitol Hill* (Washington, D.C.: Center for Responsive Politics, 1997), p. 1.

2. Ibid., p. 2. Figures do not include the $262 million in soft money that brings the Center's total to $2.4 billion.

3. For more detailed data, see Norman J. Ornstein, Thomas E. Mann, and Michael J. Malbin, *Vital Statistics on Congress 1997–1998* (Washington, D.C.: Congressional Quarterly, 1998), Table 3-9.

4. Anthony Corrado, "The Changing Environment of Presidential Campaign Finance," in William G. Mayer, ed., *In Pursuit of the White House* (Chatham, N.J.: Chatham House, 1995), p. 226.

5. Herbert E. Alexander, *Financing Politics* (Washington, D.C.: Congressional Quarterly, 1976), p. 8.

6. Makinson, *The Big Picture*, p. 2.

7. Alexander and Corrado, *Financing the 1992 Election*, p. 8.

8. Makinson, *The Big Picture*, p. 2; and Don Van Natta, Jr., "Democratic Committee Skimmed Money to Aid Clinton, Data Show," *New York Times*, September 10, 1997, p. A21.

9. Sidney Verba, Kay Lehman Schlozman, and Henry E. Brady, *Voice and Equality: Civic Voluntarism in American Politics* (Cambridge, Mass.: Harvard University Press, 1995), pp. 134–36.

10. Figures here and in the paragraphs that follow based on the author's calculations from data available from the Federal Election Commission.

11. See, for example, Makinson, *The Big Picture*, pp. 2–3; Burt Neuborne, *The Values of Campaign Finance Reform* (New York: Brennan Center for Justice, 1997); Edward B. Foley, "Equal-Dollars-Per-Voter: A Constitutional Principle of Campaign Finance," *Columbia Law Review* 94:4 (May 1994): 1204–57; and Ellen S. Miller, "Clean Elections, How To," *The American Prospect*, January–February 1997, pp. 56–59.

12. Based on data reported by the Federal Election Commission as of November 23, 1998.

13. Federal Election Commission, "PAC Activity Increases in 1995–96 Election Cycle," press release, April 22, 1997.

14. Based on the data reported in Federal Election Commission, "FEC Reports on Congressional Fundraising for 1997–98."

15. Frank J. Sorauf, *Inside Campaign Finance* (New Haven: Yale University Press, 1992), pp. 104–9.

16. The data in this table included all contributions made by PACs to federal candidates during 1997 and 1998. They thus include almost $10 million in contributions made during this period but applicable to a 1996 election campaign or contributions made to Senate candidates not up for election in 1998. These contributions are not included in the earlier PAC data that report contributions made to candidates seeking election in the 1997–98 election cycle.

17. John R. Wright, *Interest Groups and Congress* (Boston: Allyn and Bacon, 1996), pp. 128–29.

18. See, among others, Philip M. Stern, *The Best Congress Money Can Buy* (New York: Pantheon Books, 1988); Dan Clawson, Alan Neustadtl, and Denise Scott, *Money Talks: Corporate PACs and Political Influence* (New York: Basic Books, 1992); Nancy Watzman and Sheila Krumholz, *Down on the Farm: Agricultural Interests and the 1995 Farm Bill* (Washington, D.C.: Center for Responsive Politics, 1995) and *The Best Defense* (Washington, D.C.: Center for Responsive Politics, 1995).

19. Makinson, *The Big Picture*, pp. 9–10.

20. Thomas Stratmann, "The Market for Congressional Votes: Is Timing of Contributions Everything?" *Journal of Law and Economics* 41 (April 1998), pp. 85–113.

21. Peter Levine, "Expert Analysis vs. Public Opinion: The Case of Campaign Finance Reform," *Philosophy and Public Policy* 17:3 (Summer 1997): 2–3.

22. Makinson, *The Big Picture*, p. 4.

23. Unless otherwise noted, the figures provided here and in the remainder of this section are drawn from the data reported in Federal Election Commission, "1996 Congressional Financial Activity Continues Climb," press release, December 31, 1996.

24. Norman J. Ornstein, Thomas E. Mann, and Michael J. Malbin, *Vital Statistics on Congress 1995–1996* (Washington, D.C.: Congressional Quarterly, 1996), pp. 97–99; and Federal Election Commission, "1994 Congressional Spending Sets Record," press release, December 22, 1994, p. 13.

25. Federal Election Commission, "Congressional Campaign Receipts Continue to Increase, Up $125 Million over Previous Election Cycle," press release, June 5, 2000, p. 1.

26. Rachel Van Dongen, "No Garden Party in N.J.," *Roll Call*, June 5, 2000, p. 11.

27. Federal Election Commission, "FEC Reports on Congressional Fundraising for 1997–98."

28. Alexander, "Spending in the 1996 Elections," p. 18, and Makinson, *The Big Picture*, p. 4.

29. Jennifer Steen, "Self-Financing Candidates Scare Off Competitors," *Public Affairs Report* (Institute of Governmental Studies, Berkeley), September 1999, p. 11. The study also can be found at http://papers.tcnj.edu/papers/034/034015SteenJenni.pdf.

30. Ibid.

31. Data in this paragraph based on the figures reported in Norman J. Ornstein et al., *Vital Statistics on Congress, 1984–1985* (Washington, D.C.: American Enterprise Institute, 1984), p. 65, and Federal Election Commission, "FEC Reports on Congressional Fundraising for 1997–98."

32. Results reported in "Political Reform," *Washington Post*, November 10, 1992.

33. Center for Responsive Politics, "Money and Incumbency Win Big on Election Day," press release, November 4, 1998, p. 1.

34. See Alan Gerber, "Estimating the Effect of Campaign Spending on Senate Election Outcomes Using Instrumental Variables," *American Political Science Review* 92:2 (June 1998): 401–11.

35. Michael J. Malbin, "Campaign Finance Reform: Some Lessons from the Data," *Rockefeller Institute Bulletin*, 1993, p. 49.

36. Committee for Economic Development, *Investing in the People's Business: A Business Proposal for Campaign Finance Reform* (New York: Committee for Economic Development, 1999), pp. 17–18.

37. Federal Election Commission, "FEC Reports on Congressional Fundraising for 1997–98."

38. Jonathan S. Krasno and Donald Philip Green, "Stopping the Buck Here: The Case for Campaign Spending Limits," *The Brookings Review*, Spring 1993, pp. 17–21.

39. See, among others, Committee for Economic Development, *Investing in the People's Business*; and Task Force on Campaign Finance Reform, *New Realities, New Thinking* (Los Angeles: Citizens' Research Foundation, 1997).

CHAPTER 5

1. Federal Election Commission, "FEC Announces 1996 Presidential Spending Limits," press release, March 15, 1996.

2. Herbert E. Alexander, "Financing the 1996 Election," in Regina Dougherty et al., eds., *America at the Polls 1996* (Storrs, Conn.: Roper Center for Public Opinion Research, 1997), p. 146.

3. Joseph E. Cantor, *The Presidential Election Campaign Fund and Tax Checkoff: Background and Current Issues*, Congressional Research Service Report 95-824 GOV (Washington, D.C.: Library of Congress, March 1997), p. 3.

4. Federal Election Commission, "Insufficient Public Funds Still Predicted for 2000 Election," *Record* 24:7 (July 1998): 5.

5. Federal Election Commission, "Estimates of Deposits and Payouts to the Fund" (memorandum from James Pehrkon to Robert J. Costa, March 12, 1999).

6. Federal Election Commission, "FEC Approves Matching Funds for 2000 Presidential Candidates," press release, December 22, 1999.

7. Anthony Corrado, *Paying for Presidents* (New York: Twentieth Century Fund Press, 1993), pp. 16–22.

8. "Status of the Presidential Election Campaign Fund" (memorandum to the Federal Election Commission from John Surina, January 23, 1998).

9. Alexander and Corrado, *Financing the 1992 Election*, pp. 9, 11–12.

10. Robert J. Samuelson, "A Great Leap Backward," *Newsweek*, April 19, 1999, p. 47.

11. Corrado, *Paying for Presidents*, pp. 32–33.

12. Samuelson, "A Great Leap Backward."

13. Federal Election Commission, "Insufficient Public Funds Still Predicted," p. 5.

14. Ibid., p. 128; and Makinson, *The Big Picture*, p. 7.

15. For a broader discussion of the figures in this paragraph, see Corrado, "The Changing Environment of Presidential Campaign Finance," pp. 224–35.

16. Herbert E. Alexander, "Yes: Public Financing Is a Desirable Policy," in Gary L. Rose, ed., *Controversial Issues in Presidential Selection* (Albany: State University of New York Press, 1991), pp. 159–60.

17. Phil Kuntz, "Fund-Raising Race Is Also Part of Presidential Contest," *Wall Street Journal*, March 11, 1999, p. A24; and Linda Feldman, "The Race Before the Race—It's a Money Thing," *Christian Science Monitor*, April 23, 1999.

18. Corrado, "The Changing Environment of Presidential Campaign Finance," p. 242.

19. Stephen Labaton, "Limited Cash Likely to Restrict Dole's Campaign Message," *New York Times*, May 16, 1996, p. A6; and Michael Kranish, "Dole Bemoans Preconvention Spending Limits," *Boston Globe*, July 14, 1996, p. 7.

20. These activities include the financing of a media campaign to announce an individual's intention to seek a party's presidential nomination, the use of a PAC to qualify an individual for state ballots, and materials that describe an individual as a future presidential candidate. For a more detailed discussion, see Corrado, *Creative Campaigning*.

21. Ibid., Chapter 4.

22. Ruth Marcus, "Staying Ahead of the PACs," *Washington Post*, November 25, 1997, p. A1.

CHAPTER 6

1. Federal Election Commission, "15-Month Fundraising Figures of Major Parties Detailed," press release, June 20, 2000, p. 1.

2. "Memorandum in Support of the Colorado Party's Motion for Summary Judgment," *Federal Election Commission v. Colorado Republican Federal Campaign Committee*, Civil Action No. 89-N-1159, January 22, 1998, p. 26.

3. Federal Election Commission, "Soft Money: Draft Notice of Proposed Rulemaking" (memorandum to the Federal Election Commission from Lawrence M. Noble, Agenda Document 98-10, January 26, 1998), p. 22.

4. The Campaign Finance Reform study results are reported in Committee for Economic Development, *Investing in the People's Business*, p. 26, and also can be found at http://206.239.183.87/SoftMoneyReport.htm (viewed January 9, 1999).

5. Ralph Vartabedian, "Corporate Traffic Heavy on U.S. Political Money Trail," *Los Angeles Times*, September 21, 1997, p. A1.

6. Jennifer Keen and John Daly, *Beyond the Limits: Soft Money in the 1996 Elections* (Washington, D.C.: Center for Responsive Politics, 1997), pp. 3–6. It is important to note that these figures combine donations made from corporate treasury funds and individual contributions made by executives or employees of particular corporations. Similarly, the labor figures combine the sums donated from labor union treasuries with sums donated by individual executives and members of a union.

7. The examples that follow are based on the soft money contribution data found in Keen and Daly, *Beyond the Limits*.

8. Herrnson, *Congressional Elections*, p. 76. For example, in the 1996 election cycle, approximately 50 percent of the Democratic Congressional Campaign Committee's funds and 45 percent of the Democratic Senatorial Campaign Committee's funds were used to pay for computers, salaries, fundraising, media studios, and loan payments. The National Republican Congressional Committee and National Republican Senatorial Committee spent approximately 55 percent and 48 percent, respectively, on these activities.

9. The data in this paragraph and in the analysis that follows are based on the author's computations from data reported to the Federal Election Commission. See Federal Election Commission, "FEC Reports Major Increase in Party Activity for 1995–96," press release, March 19, 1997.

10. 116 S.Ct. 2309 (1996).

11. Dwyre, "Pushing the Campaign Finance Envelope," p. 15.

12. Federal Election Commission, "FEC Reports on Political Party Activity for 1997–98," press release, April 9, 1999, p.1.

13. Ibid.

14. Herrnson, *Congressional Elections*, 2nd ed., pp. 94–95.

15. Ibid.

16. For a description of how this ratio is calculated, see 11 C.F.R. §106.5(d).

17. See, among others, Susan B. Glasser, "'Soft Money' Paves the Way," *Washington Post National Weekly Edition*, October 25, 1999, pp. 6–8; Juliet Eilperin, "'The Hammer' DeLay Whips the Lobbyists into Shape," *Washington Post National Weekly Edition*, October 25, 1999, pp. 8–9; and William M. Welch and Jim Drinkard, "Rangel Emerges as Fundraising Life of the Party," *USA Today*, June 8, 2000, p. 6A.

18. Derrick Cain, "Democrats Create Seven New Committees to Move More Soft Money into Senate Races," *BNA Money and Politics Report*, December 23, 1999, p. 1.

19. David E. Rosenbaum, "Oilman Says He Got 'Access' by Giving Democrats Money," *New York Times*, September 19, 1997, p. A1; Gregory L. Vistica and Michael Isikoff, "A Shadowy Scandal," *Newsweek*, March 31, 1997, p. 34; "Georgia Republic Releases Democratic Donor Tamraz," *Washington Post*, June 17, 1997, p. A4; "Clinton Aide Questioned about Help to Party Donor," *Boston Globe*, June 5, 1997, p. A28.

20. Keen and Daly, *Beyond the Limits*, p. 19.

21. Letter from the National Republican Senatorial Committee signed by Senator Mitch McConnell, as reported in *National Journal*, October 4, 1997, p. 1957.

22. Helen Dewar and John E. Yang, "Senators Push Tobacco Tax Credit Repeal," *Washington Post*, September 10, 1997, p. A9; Helen Dewar, "Senate Votes 95-3 to Repeal $50 Billion Tobacco Tax Break," *Washington Post*, September 11, 1997, p. A1; Ceci Connolly and John E. Yang, "House Votes to Kill Break for Tobacco," *Washington Post*, September 18, 1997, p. A6.

23. "'Soft Money' Talks," *New York Times*, October 20, 1997, p. A22.

24. Brent Thompson, "Despite Reform Frenzy, Don't Blame Soft Money for Campaign Scandal," *Roll Call*, March 27, 1997, p. 12.

CHAPTER 7

1. See the District Court's opinion in *Buckley* v. *Valeo* at 519 F. 2d 869–78 (D.C. Cir., 1975) and the Supreme Court's decision at 424 U.S. 44, note 52.

2. For a review of these decisions, see Potter, "Issue Advocacy and Express Advocacy," pp. 227–70.

3. *Federal Election Commission* v. *Furgatch*, 807 F.2d 857 (9th Cir., 1987) at 864.

4. *Federal Register* 60 (July 6, 1995): 35304–5.

5. *Maine Right to Life Committee, Inc.* v. *Federal Election Commission*, 914 F. Supp. 8 (D. Me., 1996).

6. Bob Woodward, *The Choice* (New York: Simon and Schuster, 1996), p. 344; Eleanor Randolph, "Clinton Camp Sows Televised Seeds of Support in Key Regions," *Los Angeles Times*, May 22, 1996, p. 5; Common Cause, "Statement of

Common Cause President Ann McBride at News Conference Asking for Independent Counsel," press release, October 9, 1996, p. 7; Annenberg Public Policy Center, *Issue Advocacy Advertising during the 1996 Campaign: A Catalog*, Report Series No. 16 (Philadelphia: Annenberg Public Policy Center, September 1997), p. 32.

7. Julie Kosterlitz, "Laboring Uphill," *National Journal*, March 2, 1996, p. 476; Annenberg Public Policy Center, *Issue Advocacy Advertising*, p. 10; Anthony Corrado, "Financing the 1996 Elections," in Gerald M. Pomper, ed., *The Election of 1996* (Chatham, N.J.: Chatham House, 1997), p. 163.

8. Republican National Committee, "RNC Announces $20 Million TV Advertising Campaign," press release, May 16, 1996, p. 1.

9. Herrnson, *Congressional Elections*, p. 97; Annenberg Public Policy Center, *Issue Advocacy Advertising*, p. 54.

10. Eliza Newlin Carney, "Stealth Bombers," *National Journal*, August 16, 1997, p. 1642.

11. Annenberg Public Policy Center, *Issue Advocacy Advertising*, p. 27.

12. Ibid., p. 23; Carney, "Stealth Bombers," p. 1640.

13. Richard Benedetto, "Christian Coalition Saving Its Strength for Local Races," *USA Today*, October 18, 1996, p. 9A.

14. Annenberg Public Policy Center, *Issue Advocacy Advertising*, p. 7.

15. The 1998 Annenberg Public Policy Center report is available at http://appcpenn.org/issueads/report.htm.

16. Ibid.

17. http://appcpenn.org/issueads/profiles/rnc.htm.

18. Richard L. Berke, "Financial Debate Divides Democrats as Elections Near," *New York Times*, October 27, 1998, p. A14.

19. Annenberg Public Policy Center, *Issue Advocacy Advertising*, p. 3.

20. http://appcpenn.org/issueads/report.htm.

21. David B. Magleby and Marianne Holt, eds., *Outside Money: Soft Money and Issue Ads in Competitive 1998 Congressional Elections*, a report of a grant funded by the Pew Charitable Trusts (Provo, Utah: Brigham Young University, 1998), p. 196.

22. Lillian R. BeVier, "The Issue of Issue Advocacy: An Economic, Political and Constitutional Analysis," *Virginia Law Review* 85 (November 1999): 1761–92.

23. Bradley A. Smith, "The Siren's Song: Campaign Finance Regulation and the First Amendment," *Journal of Law and Policy* 6 (1997): 33.

24. For background on Section 527 and its development, see Milton Cerny and Frances R. Hill, "Political Organizations," *Tax Notes*, April 29, 1996, p. 651; and Common Cause, *Under the Radar: The Attack of "Stealth PACs" on our Nation's Elections* (Washington, D.C., 2000), pp. 1–4.

25. Common Cause, *Under the Radar*, pp. 7–9.

26. Public Law No. 106-230. This legislation, designated H.R. 4762 in both the House and the Senate, was signed into law by President Bill Clinton on July 1, 2000.

CHAPTER 8

1. For a brief summary of these previous efforts, see "Eighteen Years of Stalemate," *Congressional Quarterly Weekly Report*, October 11, 1997, p. 2450; and Helen Dewar, "Campaign Reform's Uphill Fight," *Washington Post*, October 7, 1997, p. A5.

2. For a summary of the various proposals presented after 1996, see Joseph E. Cantor, *Campaign Finance Legislation in the 105th Congress*, Congressional Research Service Report 97-324 GOV (Washington, D.C.: Library of Congress, November 26, 1997).

3. The bill was submitted in the 106th Congress as H.R. 1922, "The Citizen Legislature and Political Freedom Act."

4. Jan Witold Baran and Allison R. Hayward, "Do It Virginia's Way," *The Weekly Standard*, February 23, 1998, pp. 17–19.

5. See, for example, Bradley A. Smith, "Soft Money, Hard Realities: The Constitutional Prohibition on a Soft Money Ban," *Journal of Legislation* 24 (1998): 179–200; and David M. Mason, "Why Congress Can't Ban Soft Money," Heritage Foundation Backgrounder No. 1130, Washington, D.C., July 21, 1997.

6. The campaign finance reform proposal sponsored by Senators John McCain (R-Arizona) and Russell Feingold (D-Wisconsin), which is entitled "The Bipartisan Campaign Reform Act," was introduced as S. 25 in the 105th Congress and S. 26 in the 106th Congress. The House version sponsored by Republican Christopher Shays of Connecticut and Democrat Martin Meehan of Massachusetts was introduced as H.R. 3526 in the 105th Congress and H.R. 417 in the 106th Congress.

7. See, among others, Paul S. Herrnson, *Campaign Finance Reform and Political Parties* (Los Angeles: Citizens' Research Foundation, September 1998), pp. 2–6.

8. Jeffrey Taylor and Glenn R. Simpson, "New Idea on Campaign Finance Emerges from Defeat," *Wall Street Journal*, November 4, 1999, p. A32.

9. Hagel's proposal, S. 1816, was introduced in the 106th Congress as "The Open and Accountable Campaign Financing Act of 2000."

10. Bush for President Committee, "Governor Bush Announces Campaign Finance Reform Proposal to Ban Lobbyists from Giving while Congress Is in Session," press release, February 15, 2000; and Frank Bruni, "Bush Offers Plan on Financing of Campaigns," *New York Times*, February 16, 2000.

11. This bill, H.R. 2183, was introduced by Republican Asa Hutchinson of Arkansas and Democrat Tom Allen of Maine as "The Bipartisan Campaign Integrity Act."

12. See, for example, Ellen S. Miller, "Trojan Reform: Beware of Geeks Bearing Gifts," *Roll Call*, September 10, 1997.

13. See *Federal Register* 60 (July 6, 1995), pp. 35304–5; and Potter, "Issue Advocacy and Express Advocacy," pp. 235–36.

14. BeVier, "The Issue of Issue Advocacy," p. 1789.

15. See Anthony Corrado, "On the Issue of Issue Advocacy: A Comment," *Virginia Law Review* 85 (November 1999): 1809–12.

16. Ibid., pp. 1811–12.

17. 487 U.S. 735 (1988).

18. 320 NLRB No. 11 (1995).

19. Senate Amendment No. 1309 to S. 25 (offered October 7, 1997).

20. These provisions were included in the original bill, S. 25, that was submitted by McCain and Feingold in the 105th Congress before it was modified to focus on soft money and issue advocacy. In the House, Shays and Meehan introduced these reforms in a separate bill, H.R. 1777, which was then titled "The Campaign Independence Restoration Act, Part II." The soft money and issue advocacy reforms were originally submitted in the 105th Congress by Shays and Meehan as the symbolic H.R. 1776, then titled "The Campaign Independence Restoration Act, Part I."

21. For background on this approach to reform, see David Donnelly, Janice Fine, and Ellen S. Miller, *Money and Politics: Financing Our Elections Democratically* (Boston: Beacon Press, 1999); and Miller, "Clean Elections, How To." A full public funding proposal for federal elections has been submitted in the 106th Congress as S. 982, "The Clean Money, Clean Elections Act."

22. *Daggett v. Webster*, No. 98-223 (D. Maine, November 5, 1999).

23. The discussion that follows is based on "Gore Proposes New 'Democracy Endowment' and Other Measures to Help Reduce Influence of Money in Politics," Gore 2000 press release, March 27, 2000; Katharine Q. Seelye, "Gore Proposing Endowment Fund to Pay for Political Campaigns," *New York Times*, March 27, 2000, p. A1; and Ceci Connolly, "Finance Plan May Only Reform Gore's Image," *Washington Post*, March 28, 2000, p. A6.

INDEX

Note: Page numbers followed by letters *n* and *t* refer to notes and tables, respectively.

ABOUT THE AUTHOR

A nthony Corrado, an associate professor of government at Colby College, has extensive practical experience in the management and financing of presidential campaigns, serving on the staffs of the past three Democrat presidential nominees, and as a consultant for delegate and convention operations for the Clinton for President Committee. He is the author of numerous articles on presidential campaign finance and the Federal Election Campaign Act as well as a number of books, including *Creative Campaigning: PACs and the Presidential Selection Process* (1992) and *Paying for Presidents: Public Financing in National Election* (1993), coauthor (with Herbert E. Alexander) of *Financing the 1992 Election* (1995), and editor of *Campaign Finance Reform: A Sourcebook* (1997) and *Elections in Cyberspace: Toward a New Era in American Politics* (forthcoming).